Disclaimer

This book provides general information about intellectual property law and practices in the United States. It is intended for educational and informational purposes only and should not be considered legal advice. While every effort has been made to ensure the accuracy and completeness of the information contained in this book, intellectual property laws and regulations are subject to change, and their application can vary depending on specific circumstances.

Readers are encouraged to seek professional legal counsel for advice specific to their individual situations or for guidance on any particular legal matter related to intellectual property. The authors, publishers, and contributors of this book disclaim any liability or responsibility for any errors, omissions, or outcomes resulting from the use of this information. This book does not create an attorney-client relationship, and the use of this book or reliance on its content is at the reader's own risk. Always consult with a qualifie attorney before making any decisions regarding intellectual property rights or related legal matters.

Table of Contents

Introduction:

Navigating Intellectual Property in the Digital Age

Intellectual property (IP) is a cornerstone of innovation and economic growth, providing legal protection for creations of the mind—such as inventions, literary and artistic works, designs, symbols, names, and images. In today's fast-paced and digitally connected world, IP is more valuable and more vulnerable than ever. As businesses, entrepreneurs, and creators increasingly rely on digital platforms to share, distribute, and monetize their work, they face new challenges in protecting their IP rights.

The United States offers a robust legal framework for IP protection, but the rapid evolution of technology and the global nature of the internet create complexities that require careful navigation. Understanding how to manage and safeguard IP in the digital environment is crucial for maintaining competitive advantage, ensuring legal compliance, and protecting valuable assets from infringement.

This book provides a comprehensive guide to navigating the complexities of IP in the United States, with a focus on the digital landscape. From identifying the different types of IP and their respective protections to filing and registration procedures, classification methods, and handling confidential information, each chapter offers practical insights and strategies for effective IP management.

We delve into key topics such as avoiding infringements, defending against claims, utilizing IP on the internet, and maintaining and monitoring IP rights. The book also covers essential tools and techniques for digital monitoring, responding to online violations, and staying informed about legal changes. Whether you are an entrepreneur, business owner, legal professional, or creator, this guide equips you with the knowledge needed to protect your IP in an ever-evolving digital world.

By understanding the foundational principles of IP law, implementing best practices for digital protection, and leveraging the right tools and strategies, you can navigate the complexities of IP management with confidence and clarity. This book is your resource for mastering the art of protecting your intellectual property in the 21st century.

Chapter 1:

Identifying the Types of Intellectual Property in the United States

Copyright

Copyright is a form of legal protection granted to the creators of original works of authorship. This protection is rooted in the U.S. Constitution, which empowers Congress to promote the progress of science and useful arts by securing exclusive rights for authors and inventors. Here is a detailed exploration of what copyright entails in the United States, including its definition, scope, duration, rights, and limitations.

Definition and Legal Basis

Copyright in the United States is governed by Title 17 of the U.S. Code, which defines copyright as the protection provided to "original works of authorship" that are fixed in a tangible medium of expression. To be eligible for copyright, a work must meet three primary criteria:

- **Originality**: The work must be independently created by the author and possess at least some minimal degree of creativity. Originality does not require novelty or uniqueness but must not be copied from another source.
- **Work of Authorship**: The work must fall into one of the recognized categories, such as literary, musical, dramatic, choreographic, pictorial, graphic, sculptural, audiovisual, sound recordings, and architectural works.
- **Fixed in a Tangible Medium**: The work must be fixed in a tangible medium of expression, meaning it is embodied in a physical or digital form that is sufficiently stable to be perceived, reproduced, or otherwise communicated for more than a transitory period (e.g., written on paper, recorded on a CD, saved on a computer).

The legal framework for copyright is established under the Copyright Act of 1976, which has been amended several times to address new challenges posed by technological advances. The Act provides a comprehensive set of rules regarding what is protected, the rights granted, and the exceptions to those rights.

Types of Works Protected

Copyright protection extends to a wide range of creative works, each with unique attributes and requirements for protection:

- **Literary Works**: Includes fiction, non-fiction, poetry, articles, essays, and computer programs. The protection covers the text's expression, not the ideas, systems, or procedures it describes.
- **Musical Works**: Compositions with or without accompanying words, including notated music and lyrics. Copyright protects the combination of melody, harmony, and rhythm.
- **Dramatic Works**: Plays, scripts, screenplays, and similar works intended for performance. The protection includes dialogue, stage directions, and plot development but not the performance itself unless it is recorded.
- **Choreographic Works**: Original choreographed routines, which must be recorded or otherwise documented to receive protection. This category covers ballet, dance, and other forms of choreographed movement.
- **Pictorial, Graphic, and Sculptural Works**: Paintings, drawings, photographs, sculptures, maps, charts, and models. The protection covers the visual expression of ideas, not the ideas themselves.
- **Audiovisual Works**: Works consisting of a series of related images intended to be shown with accompanying sounds, such as movies, television shows, and videos.
- **Sound Recordings**: Works resulting from the fixation of a series of musical, spoken, or other sounds. The protection covers the recording, not the composition or lyrics unless those elements are separately protected.
- **Architectural Works**: The design of buildings as embodied in architectural plans, drawings, or constructed buildings.

4

Protection extends to the overall form and arrangement of the design elements but not to standard features or utilitarian aspects.

Duration of Protection

The duration of copyright protection depends on several factors, including when the work was created, the type of work, and whether the work was created by an individual, jointly by multiple authors, or as a "work for hire."

- Works Created on or After January 1, 1978: Copyright protection lasts for the life of the author plus 70 years. For joint works, the protection lasts for 70 years after the death of the last surviving author.
- Works for Hire, Anonymous, or Pseudonymous Works: Protection lasts for 95 years from the date of first publication or 120 years from the date of creation, whichever is shorter.
- Works Created Before January 1, 1978: These works are governed by the rules that applied before the Copyright Act of 1976. Generally, they are protected for 95 years from the date of publication if the copyright was renewed properly.
- Special Considerations for "Works for Hire": A work for hire is created by an employee within the scope of their employment or specifically commissioned work that falls under specific categories (e.g., a contribution to a collective work, a part of a motion picture, a translation). In these cases, the employer or commissioning party is considered the copyright owner, and the duration is 95 or 120 years.

Rights Granted to Copyright Holders

Copyright law grants the copyright holder a bundle of exclusive rights that enable the owner to control and exploit their work economically. These rights include:

- Reproduction Right: The right to reproduce the work in copies or phonorecords, allowing the copyright owner to control who can make copies and distribute them.
- Distribution Right: The right to distribute copies or phonorecords of the work to the public by sale, transfer of ownership, rental,

lease, or lending. This right includes the "first sale doctrine," which limits the copyright owner's control after the initial authorized sale.

- Public Performance Right: The right to perform the work publicly, including live performances, broadcasts, and transmissions to the public. This right applies to literary, musical, dramatic, and choreographic works, as well as audiovisual works.
- Public Display Right: The right to display the work publicly, whether directly or by means of a film, slide, or other device. This right covers pictorial, graphic, and sculptural works.
- Derivative Works Right: The right to prepare derivative works based on the original, such as adaptations, translations, or dramatizations. This allows the copyright holder to control modifications that represent a transformation of the original work.
- Digital Transmission Right: For sound recordings, the right to perform the work publicly by means of a digital audio transmission, which includes streaming over the internet.

Limitations and Exceptions

While copyright grants exclusive rights, it also includes several important limitations and exceptions that balance the rights of the creator with public interest:

- **Fair Use**: A critical limitation that allows the use of copyrighted material without permission under certain conditions, such as for purposes of criticism, comment, news reporting, teaching, scholarship, or research. Courts evaluate fair use based on four factors: purpose and character of the use (including whether it's commercial or educational), nature of the copyrighted work, amount and substantiality of the portion used, and effect on the market value of the original work.
- **Public Domain**: Works not protected by copyright because the term has expired, the work was never eligible for copyright, or the author waived their rights. Works in the public domain can be freely used by anyone.

- **First Sale Doctrine**: The principle that allows the purchaser of a legally obtained copy of a copyrighted work to resell, lend, or dispose of that copy without the copyright holder's permission. This doctrine is particularly relevant to physical books, music, and art.
- **Specific Statutory Exemptions**: These include exemptions for libraries and archives for preservation, exemptions for certain educational performances and displays, and exemptions for certain uses by people with disabilities (e.g., making works accessible in braille or other formats).
- **Compulsory Licenses**: Situations where the law requires the copyright holder to license their work, often under regulated terms. Examples include mechanical licenses for cover songs and statutory licenses for retransmission of broadcast signals.
- **Safe Harbor Provisions**: Digital Millennium Copyright Act (DMCA) provisions that protect internet service providers (ISPs) and online platforms from liability for user-generated content, provided they follow specific guidelines like promptly removing infringing material upon notice.

By understanding these aspects of copyright, individuals and businesses can better navigate their rights and responsibilities under U.S. law, ensuring their creative works are protected while respecting the balance between private rights and public access.

Patents

Patents are a form of intellectual property protection that grants the patent holder exclusive rights to an invention, providing legal protection against others making, using, selling, or importing the invention without permission. Patents are designed to encourage innovation by providing inventors with a limited period of exclusive rights in exchange for publicly disclosing the details of their invention.

Definition and Legal Basis

In the United States, patents are governed by Title 35 of the U.S. Code, which defines the scope, requirements, and procedures for obtaining patent protection. Patents are granted by the United States Patent and Trademark Office (USPTO) and are categorized into three main types:

- **Utility Patents**: The most common type of patent, granted for new and useful processes, machines, articles of manufacture, or compositions of matter, or any new and useful improvement thereof. Examples include software algorithms, mechanical devices, and pharmaceutical compositions.
- **Design Patents**: Granted for new, original, and ornamental designs for an article of manufacture. Design patents protect the unique visual qualities (appearance) of a manufactured item, not its functional aspects. Examples include the shape of a bottle, the pattern of a fabric, or the appearance of a smartphone.
- **Plant Patents**: Granted to anyone who invents or discovers and asexually reproduces a distinct and new variety of plant. Asexual reproduction refers to methods like grafting or cutting, where the plant is reproduced without seeds. Plant patents are typically granted for new varieties of flowers, fruits, or other plants.

The primary legal foundation for patents in the U.S. is established under the Patent Act, which has been amended numerous times to adapt to technological advances and evolving public policy considerations. The America Invents Act (AIA) of 2011 is a significant reform that introduced the "first-to-file" system, aligning the U.S. patent process more closely with international practices.

Requirements for Patentability

To qualify for a patent, an invention must meet specific criteria established by the USPTO. The main requirements for patentability are:

- **Novelty**: The invention must be new and not previously disclosed in any prior art. Prior art includes any public knowledge, prior publications, patents, or other publicly available information about the invention before the filing date. If an invention is already known or published, it cannot be patented. Under the AIA, the U.S. follows a "first-to-file" system, meaning that the first person to file a patent application, not necessarily the first to invent, is entitled to the patent rights.

- **Non-Obviousness**: The invention must not be obvious to a person of ordinary skill in the relevant field at the time of the invention. This means that the invention should involve an inventive step or a level of creativity beyond what is considered common knowledge in the field. The USPTO assesses non-obviousness by examining whether combining prior art references would have made the invention predictable to someone skilled in the art.
- **Usefulness (Utility)**: The invention must have a specific, substantial, and credible utility. It must perform a useful function and have a real-world application. The usefulness requirement is generally easy to satisfy, but the invention must provide a practical benefit, not be frivolous or trivial.
- **Full and Clear Disclosure**: The patent application must include a written description of the invention that is full, clear, concise, and exact enough to enable a person skilled in the art to make and use the invention. This requirement ensures that the invention is adequately disclosed to the public in exchange for the patent's exclusive rights. The application must also include any drawings necessary to understand the invention and disclose the "best mode" of carrying out the invention, although the AIA removed the failure to disclose the best mode as grounds for invalidating a patent.

Duration of Protection

The duration of a patent's protection depends on the type of patent granted:

- **Utility Patents**: Utility patents are granted for 20 years from the filing date of the patent application. To maintain a utility patent, the patent holder must pay maintenance fees at specific intervals (3.5, 7.5, and 11.5 years after the patent is granted). Failure to pay these fees can result in the patent's expiration before the end of the 20-year term.
- **Design Patents**: Design patents are granted for 15 years from the grant date, without the requirement for maintenance fees. The

term length for design patents was extended from 14 to 15 years by the Patent Law Treaties Implementation Act of 2012.

- **Plant Patents**: Plant patents are granted for 20 years from the filing date, similar to utility patents. However, unlike utility patents, there are no maintenance fees required to keep plant patents in force.

It is essential to note that patent rights are territorial, meaning a U.S. patent only provides protection within the United States and its territories. To obtain patent protection in other countries, separate applications must be filed in each desired jurisdiction, often through international treaties like the Patent Cooperation Treaty (PCT).

Rights Granted to Patent Holders

A patent grants the patent holder a set of exclusive rights for a limited period, which allows them to control the use of their invention and potentially monetize it. The key rights conferred to a patent holder include:

- **Right to Exclude Others from Making**: The patent holder has the exclusive right to manufacture the patented invention. If a third party makes the invention without the patent holder's permission, the patent holder can sue for infringement.
- **Right to Exclude Others from Using**: The patent holder can prevent others from using the invention, which can be particularly important for process patents or patents covering unique methods or software algorithms.
- **Right to Exclude Others from Selling or Offering for Sale**: The patent holder has the right to control the commercialization of the invention, including its sale or offer for sale. Unauthorized sales or offers to sell the invention can lead to legal action.
- **Right to Exclude Others from Importing**: The patent holder can prevent the unauthorized importation of products that incorporate the patented invention into the U.S. market.

These rights are enforceable in court, and the patent holder can seek remedies such as injunctions to stop infringing activities, monetary damages for past infringement, and potentially enhanced damages if the infringement is deemed willful.

Patentability vs. Unpatentable Subject Matter

While patents cover a wide range of inventions, certain types of subject matter cannot be patented, even if they meet the basic criteria of novelty, non-obviousness, and utility. The following are examples of unpatentable subject matter under U.S. law:

- **Abstract Ideas**: Concepts that are purely abstract, such as mathematical formulas, algorithms, or general business methods, cannot be patented unless they are applied in a specific, practical way. For example, a mathematical formula used in a software program to perform a specific function might be patentable, but the formula itself is not.
- **Natural Phenomena**: Discoveries of natural phenomena, laws of nature, or natural products cannot be patented. For example, a newly discovered plant species in the wild or a naturally occurring mineral cannot be patented, although a genetically modified plant or a synthetic version of a naturally occurring compound may be patentable.
- **Laws of Nature**: Fundamental scientific principles, such as the law of gravity or $E=mc^2$, cannot be patented. However, the application of such principles in a novel and non-obvious way may be patentable (e.g., a new machine that uses the principles of physics to achieve a new function).
- **Purely Mental Processes**: Processes that can be performed entirely in the human mind without any physical manifestation or transformation are generally not patentable. For example, a method for performing mental calculations would not be patentable.
- **Methods of Medical Treatment**: In the U.S., medical practitioners are generally shielded from liability for patent infringement when performing medical procedures. However, certain diagnostic methods and medical devices may still be patentable.

11

- **Offensive or Immoral Inventions**: In rare cases, the USPTO may refuse to grant a patent on inventions considered "contrary to public order or morality," although this is not a common ground for rejection in the U.S.

By understanding the criteria for patentability and the types of inventions that cannot be patented, inventors and businesses can better navigate the complexities of the U.S. patent system, protect their innovations, and avoid costly legal disputes over patent eligibility.

Trademarks

Trademarks are a form of intellectual property that protect symbols, words, phrases, logos, or other identifiers that distinguish the goods or services of one business from those of others. Trademarks serve as a badge of origin, helping consumers identify and differentiate products and services in the marketplace. Trademarks play a crucial role in maintaining a brand's reputation and consumer trust by ensuring that the source of a product or service remains consistent.

Definition and Legal Basis

A trademark is any word, name, symbol, design, or any combination thereof used in commerce to identify and distinguish the goods or services of one seller or provider from those of others and to indicate the source of the goods or services. In the United States, trademarks are governed by both federal law under the Lanham Act (15 U.S.C. §§ 1051 et seq.) and state laws. The Lanham Act provides the framework for registering, enforcing, and protecting trademarks at the federal level through the United States Patent and Trademark Office (USPTO).

Trademarks can protect a wide range of identifiers, including:

- **Words and Phrases**: Names, slogans, catchphrases, and other word-based identifiers (e.g., "Nike," "Just Do It").
- **Symbols and Designs**: Logos, emblems, graphic designs, and other visual symbols (e.g., the Apple logo).
- **Shapes**: Distinctive shapes of products or packaging that are non-functional (e.g., the shape of a Coca-Cola bottle).

- **Colors**: Specific colors that are used distinctively in the branding of a product or service (e.g., Tiffany & Co.'s robin egg blue).
- **Sounds**: Distinctive sounds that are associated with a brand (e.g., NBC's chimes).
- **Scents**: Unique scents that can serve as a brand identifier, though these are rare and must meet strict requirements (e.g., a specific fragrance for a product).

Types of Trademarks

Trademarks come in various forms, each serving a specific purpose in protecting brand identity. Here are the primary types of trademarks:

- **Service Marks**: A service mark is similar to a trademark but identifies and distinguishes the source of a service rather than a product. For example, "FedEx" is a service mark for delivery services. The term "trademark" is often used generically to refer to both trademarks and service marks.
- **Collective Marks**: A collective mark indicates membership in a particular organization or association. These marks are used by members of a collective group, such as a trade association, to signify their affiliation and to promote common standards. For example, the "CPA" mark is a collective mark used by members of the American Institute of Certified Public Accountants.
- **Certification Marks**: A certification mark is used by an organization to indicate that a product or service meets certain standards, such as quality, material, mode of manufacture, or geographical origin. Certification marks are not owned by the companies that use them but by an organization that verifies compliance with specific standards. For example, "UL" is a certification mark for products meeting Underwriters Laboratories standards for safety.
- **Trade Dress**: Trade dress refers to the overall visual appearance and design of a product or its packaging, including features like size, shape, color, texture, graphics, and even certain aspects of the retail environment. Trade dress protection can apply if the design is distinctive and identifies the product's source, provided

it is not functional. For example, the design and layout of an Apple store are protected as trade dress.

Duration and Renewal

One of the key advantages of trademarks over other forms of intellectual property is their potentially indefinite duration. Unlike patents or copyrights, which expire after a specific period, trademarks can last indefinitely as long as they are used in commerce and their registration is maintained through proper renewal.

- **Initial Registration Period**: In the United States, a trademark registered with the USPTO is initially valid for ten years from the date of registration.
- **Renewal Requirements**: Trademark owners must periodically file specific documents and pay fees to maintain their trademark rights. After the first five years of registration, the owner must file a Declaration of Continued Use (Section 8 Declaration) and a Renewal Application (Section 9) every ten years. This process involves submitting proof that the mark is still in use in commerce or, if not currently in use, providing a valid reason for non-use.
- **Indefinite Duration with Proper Use**: If the trademark owner continues to use the mark in commerce and complies with the renewal requirements, the trademark can remain in effect indefinitely. However, failure to file the necessary declarations and applications or ceasing the use of the mark in commerce could result in cancellation or loss of rights.

Rights Granted to Trademark Holders

A registered trademark grants the owner several exclusive rights designed to protect their brand identity and prevent consumer confusion. These rights include:

- **Exclusive Right to Use the Mark**: The owner has the exclusive right to use the trademark in connection with the goods or services for which it is registered. This prevents others from using the same or a confusingly similar mark in a way that could deceive or confuse consumers.

- **Right to License the Mark**: The owner can license the use of the trademark to others, allowing them to use it under specific conditions while retaining ownership. Licensing can provide additional revenue streams and help expand the brand's reach.
- **Right to Transfer or Sell the Mark**: The owner can assign the trademark to another party, transferring ownership rights, either in whole or in part. This is commonly done when businesses are sold or merged.
- **Right to Sue for Infringement**: If another party uses a confusingly similar mark in a way that could cause consumer confusion or dilute the brand's reputation, the trademark owner can sue for infringement. Infringement lawsuits can result in court orders to stop the infringing use (injunctions), monetary damages, and, in some cases, the recovery of legal fees.
- **Protection Against Dilution**: For famous trademarks, U.S. law provides additional protection against dilution, which occurs when a mark's distinctiveness or reputation is weakened by unauthorized use, even without consumer confusion. This protection applies to marks that are widely recognized by the public (e.g., "Coca-Cola").
- **Right to Use the ® Symbol**: Once a trademark is federally registered, the owner can use the ® symbol to indicate that the mark is registered. This symbol provides public notice of the mark's registration status and can serve as evidence of the owner's rights in legal proceedings. The ™ symbol can be used for unregistered trademarks.

Importance of Distinctiveness

Distinctiveness is a critical requirement for trademark protection. The distinctiveness of a mark determines its eligibility for registration and the strength of the protection it receives. The USPTO evaluates the distinctiveness of a trademark based on its ability to identify the source of goods or services and distinguish them from those of others. Distinctiveness is assessed along a spectrum:

- **Fanciful or Arbitrary Marks**: These are the strongest and most distinctive types of trademarks.

- Fanciful Marks: Made-up or invented words that have no meaning other than as a brand (e.g., "Kodak" or "Xerox").
  - Arbitrary Marks: Common words used in an unrelated context (e.g., "Apple" for computers). Fanciful and arbitrary marks are highly distinctive and receive strong protection.
- **Suggestive Marks**: Marks that suggest or hint at some quality or characteristic of the goods or services but require imagination or thought to understand the connection (e.g., "Netflix" for an online movie streaming service). Suggestive marks are considered inherently distinctive and are eligible for registration without proof of secondary meaning.
- **Descriptive Marks**: Marks that describe a characteristic, quality, feature, function, or purpose of the goods or services (e.g., "Cold and Creamy" for ice cream). Descriptive marks are not inherently distinctive and are generally not eligible for registration unless they have acquired secondary meaning. Secondary meaning occurs when the public has come to recognize the mark as identifying a specific source rather than merely describing the product.
- **Generic Marks**: Terms that refer to the general category or class of goods or services (e.g., "Computer" for computers). Generic marks are never eligible for trademark protection because they do not distinguish the source of the product or service; they are considered too broad to be monopolized by any one party.

The distinctiveness of a trademark is essential because it directly impacts the ability to obtain registration and enforce rights against infringers. The more distinctive a mark, the stronger the legal protection and the easier it is to defend against unauthorized use. For this reason, businesses should carefully choose and develop trademarks that are as unique and distinctive as possible to maximize their value and legal protection.

Industrial Designs

Industrial designs refer to the ornamental or aesthetic aspects of an article, which can include the shape, configuration, pattern, or color of a product. In the United States, the protection of industrial designs is primarily achieved through design patents, which provide legal rights over the visual appearance of a product rather than its functional features. Design patents play a crucial role in distinguishing products in the marketplace and can be a valuable asset for companies seeking to enhance their brand identity and product appeal.

Definition and Legal Basis

An industrial design, in the context of U.S. intellectual property law, refers to the unique visual qualities of a product that result from its design. Design patents, governed by Title 35 of the U.S. Code (specifically 35 U.S.C. § 171), protect the ornamental design of a functional item. The key elements of design patent protection include:

- **Ornamental Design**: Design patents cover the aesthetic or ornamental aspects of a functional product. This includes any new, original, and ornamental shape, configuration, or surface decoration applied to an article of manufacture. The design must be visible when the product is in use or in its normal and intended environment.
- **Scope of Protection**: The protection afforded by a design patent is limited to the specific appearance shown in the patent drawings. It does not extend to the functional aspects of the article, which may be protected by a utility patent if they meet the criteria for patentability.
- **Legal Basis**: Design patents are granted under the authority of the United States Patent and Trademark Office (USPTO), as outlined in 35 U.S.C. § 171-173. The statutory requirement is that the design must be new, original, and ornamental. It must be applied to or embodied in an article of manufacture, meaning it must be part of a tangible product.

The protection of industrial designs is critical for companies that wish to maintain a competitive edge through distinctive product appearances. Unlike copyrights or trademarks, which protect creative works and brand identifiers, design patents specifically safeguard the ornamental designs of practical objects.

Requirements for Design Protection

To qualify for design patent protection, a design must meet specific requirements set by the USPTO. The following criteria must be satisfied:

- **Novelty**: The design must be new and original, meaning it has not been publicly disclosed or used before the filing date of the patent application. This includes prior designs that are publicly known, published, sold, or used in the U.S. or abroad. The USPTO will conduct a search of prior art to ensure that the design is indeed novel.

- **Originality**: The design must originate from the applicant and not be a copy of an existing design. It must reflect the applicant's unique artistic expression and cannot be simply a reproduction or imitation of another design.

- **Ornamentality**: The design must be purely ornamental, meaning it relates to the visual qualities or aesthetics of a product rather than its functional attributes. The design cannot be dictated solely by the function of the product. For example, the unique shape or pattern on a chair may qualify for design patent protection, but the structural elements necessary for the chair's function would not.

- **Non-Obviousness**: Although the non-obviousness standard for design patents is less stringent than for utility patents, the design still must not be obvious to a designer of ordinary skill in the relevant field. If the design is a trivial modification of an existing design or merely a combination of known designs, it may be deemed obvious and thus not patentable.

- **Application Requirements**: The design patent application must include a complete description of the design, along with one or more drawings or photographs that clearly and accurately depict the appearance of the design. The drawings must show all aspects of the design from different perspectives (e.g., top, bottom, side views) to ensure full disclosure. The application must also include a claim stating that the patent is for the ornamental design as shown.

- **Single Design Requirement**: The application must be for a single design applied to a single article. If an applicant wishes to protect multiple designs or the same design applied to different articles, separate applications are typically required.

By satisfying these requirements, applicants can secure design patent protection, which grants them exclusive rights to the ornamental aspects of their products, preventing others from copying or imitating the visual appearance of their designs.

Duration of Protection

The duration of protection for a design patent in the United States is 15 years from the date of grant, as per the changes implemented by the Patent Law Treaties Implementation Act (PLTIA) of 2012. This period provides the patent holder with exclusive rights to the design for a limited time, after which the design enters the public domain.

- **No Maintenance Fees**: Unlike utility patents, design patents do not require periodic maintenance fees to keep the patent in force. Once granted, the design patent remains valid for the full 15-year term, provided the owner does not fail to comply with other legal obligations, such as timely payment of initial filing fees.
- **Scope of Duration**: The 15-year protection term is counted from the date the USPTO issues the patent, not from the filing date of the application. During this period, the patent holder can exclude others from making, using, selling, or importing the design into the United States.
- **Extensions and Limitations**: The duration of a design patent is fixed, and no extensions are available, unlike some circumstances with utility patents (e.g., patent term adjustments for delays). However, design patents can be declared invalid if they are found to have been improperly granted, such as through challenges in court or before the USPTO's Patent Trial and Appeal Board (PTAB).

Rights Granted to Design Patent Holders

Design patent holders are granted a set of exclusive rights to protect the ornamental aspects of their designs and to prevent unauthorized use by others. These rights include:

- **Right to Exclude Others from Making the Design**: The patent holder has the exclusive right to manufacture or produce products featuring the patented design. If a competitor or any other entity makes a product with a design substantially similar to the patented design, the patent holder can take legal action against them.
- **Right to Exclude Others from Using the Design**: The patent holder can prevent others from using the design in any way, including promotional activities, advertising, or other forms of use that could cause confusion in the marketplace or dilute the design's distinctiveness.
- **Right to Exclude Others from Selling or Offering for Sale**: The patent holder has the exclusive right to sell or offer for sale the products that feature the patented design. Unauthorized sales or attempts to sell such products can result in infringement claims.
- **Right to Exclude Others from Importing**: The patent holder can prevent others from importing products that embody the patented design into the United States. This right helps protect the domestic market from infringing products manufactured abroad and imported for sale.
- **Right to License the Design**: The patent holder can license the use of the design to other parties, allowing them to manufacture or sell products featuring the design in exchange for royalties or other compensation. Licensing agreements can provide a valuable revenue stream for patent holders and help expand their market reach.
- **Right to Sue for Infringement**: If a third party uses, makes, sells, or imports a design that is substantially similar to the patented design without authorization, the patent holder can sue for infringement. Remedies may include injunctive relief (court

orders to stop the infringing activity), monetary damages (including lost profits and reasonable royalties), and, in some cases, enhanced damages for willful infringement.

Design patent rights enable businesses to maintain a competitive advantage by safeguarding their unique product designs against imitation and copying. The scope of protection is limited to the ornamental features of the design as shown in the patent drawings, so enforcement and defense require careful attention to the design's specific visual characteristics.

Trade Secrets

Trade secrets are a form of intellectual property that protect confidential business information which provides a competitive edge. Unlike other forms of IP, trade secrets are not registered with a government office; instead, their protection depends on the owner's efforts to maintain their secrecy. The economic value of a trade secret lies in its confidentiality, and its unauthorized use or disclosure by others can cause significant harm to the owner.

Definition and Legal Basis

A trade secret is broadly defined as any information that:

1. **Is not generally known** or readily ascertainable by proper means by others who could obtain economic value from its disclosure or use.
2. **Derives independent economic value** from being kept secret.
3. **Is the subject of reasonable efforts** by its owner to maintain its secrecy.

The primary legal framework for trade secret protection in the United States is provided by the **Defend Trade Secrets Act (DTSA) of 2016**, which is codified under 18 U.S.C. §§ 1836-1839. The DTSA provides a federal cause of action for trade secret misappropriation, allowing owners to file civil lawsuits in federal court. This Act harmonizes trade secret protection across states and supplements state trade secret laws, which are primarily governed by versions of the Uniform Trade Secrets Act (UTSA).

Under the DTSA, a trade secret is defined as all forms and types of financial, business, scientific, technical, economic, or engineering information, including formulas, patterns, compilations, programs, devices, methods, techniques, processes, or codes, whether tangible or intangible, that:

- The owner has taken reasonable measures to keep secret.
- Derives independent economic value from not being generally known to, and not being readily ascertainable through proper means by, another person who can obtain economic value from its disclosure or use.

The DTSA aligns the United States with international standards for trade secret protection and provides various remedies, including civil seizure, damages, and injunctions, to prevent the misappropriation and misuse of trade secrets.

Types of Information Protected

Trade secrets can encompass a wide variety of confidential business information that provides a competitive advantage. The types of information that can qualify as a trade secret include, but are not limited to:

- **Formulas and Recipes**: Secret formulas for chemical compounds, pharmaceuticals, or food and beverage products (e.g., the formula for Coca-Cola or KFC's secret recipe).
- **Business Practices and Strategies**: Unique methods for conducting business operations, marketing strategies, customer lists, pricing strategies, or supplier agreements.
- **Designs and Prototypes**: Confidential product designs, blueprints, prototypes, or plans that are not yet public and provide a competitive edge.
- **Processes and Manufacturing Methods**: Proprietary processes for manufacturing, processing, or assembling products, including those involving unique technologies or techniques (e.g., a special process for manufacturing a high-strength alloy).

- **Computer Software and Algorithms**: Confidential algorithms, source code, software, or data processing methods that are critical to the operation of a company's technology or service.
- **Research and Development Data**: Experimental data, test results, and scientific or technical data collected during research and development activities, especially when leading to new product developments or innovations.
- **Financial and Commercial Information**: Confidential financial information, such as profit margins, cost structures, financial forecasts, or business plans that are not publicly disclosed.

Virtually any information that meets the criteria of being valuable due to its secrecy and being subject to reasonable efforts to maintain its secrecy can qualify as a trade secret. However, trade secrets do not include information that is generally known or easily ascertainable through public sources or independent discovery.

Duration of Protection

One of the key advantages of trade secret protection over other forms of intellectual property is that it can last indefinitely, provided the information remains secret. There is no statutory limit on the duration of trade secret protection. However, this protection is contingent upon the following conditions:

- **Continuous Secrecy**: The information must remain confidential and not become publicly known. Once a trade secret is disclosed or becomes public knowledge, whether through authorized or unauthorized means, its status as a trade secret is lost.
- **Reasonable Efforts to Maintain Secrecy**: The owner must take reasonable steps to protect the confidentiality of the trade secret. If the owner fails to implement adequate measures to safeguard the information, it may lose its status as a trade secret. Courts evaluate whether the efforts to maintain secrecy were reasonable based on factors such as the nature of the information, industry standards, and the costs and practicality of protective measures.

- **Non-Obsolescence**: The trade secret must continue to have economic value from being kept secret. If the information becomes obsolete or loses its competitive advantage (e.g., due to technological advances or changes in the market), its protection may become irrelevant, even if it remains confidential.

As long as these conditions are met, trade secret protection can remain in place indefinitely, providing a potentially perpetual form of intellectual property protection.

Rights and Enforcement

Trade secret rights are primarily enforced through civil litigation and, in certain cases, criminal prosecution. The rights associated with trade secrets and methods of enforcement under the DTSA and state laws include:

- **Right to Exclude Others from Using the Trade Secret**: The owner of a trade secret has the right to prevent others from using, disclosing, or benefiting from the trade secret without authorization.
- **Civil Remedies for Misappropriation**: Under the DTSA, an owner can file a civil lawsuit in federal court for misappropriation, seeking various remedies, including:
  - **Injunctions**: Court orders prohibiting the misappropriator from using or disclosing the trade secret.
  - **Monetary Damages**: Compensation for actual losses caused by the misappropriation, including damages for unjust enrichment or reasonable royalties for unauthorized use.
  - **Exemplary Damages**: In cases of willful and malicious misappropriation, courts may award exemplary (punitive) damages of up to twice the amount of actual damages.
  - **Attorney's Fees**: In cases of willful misappropriation or bad faith litigation, the prevailing party may be awarded reasonable attorney's fees.
- **Civil Seizure**: The DTSA allows for a unique remedy known as "civil seizure," where, in extraordinary circumstances, a court can order the seizure of property necessary to prevent the

dissemination or use of the trade secret. This remedy is typically used when there is a risk that the trade secret will be destroyed, moved, or otherwise made inaccessible.

- **Criminal Penalties**: Trade secret theft can also lead to criminal prosecution under the Economic Espionage Act (EEA) of 1996, which provides criminal penalties for individuals or entities engaged in the theft of trade secrets for economic or espionage purposes. Penalties can include fines, imprisonment, and forfeiture of assets.

- **Enforcement Against Third Parties**: Trade secret owners can also enforce their rights against third parties who knowingly receive or use misappropriated trade secrets. For example, if a competitor hires an employee who has stolen trade secrets from a former employer, both the employee and the new employer may be liable for misappropriation.

By leveraging these enforcement mechanisms, trade secret owners can protect their valuable confidential information from unauthorized use and disclosure, thereby maintaining their competitive advantage in the marketplace.

Protective Measures

To maintain trade secret protection, it is essential for the owner to implement reasonable measures to safeguard the confidentiality of the information. The following are practical tips and strategies to help protect trade secrets:

- **Confidentiality Agreements (NDAs)**: Use Non-Disclosure Agreements (NDAs) with employees, contractors, suppliers, and any other third parties who may have access to confidential information. NDAs should clearly define what constitutes a trade secret, the obligations of confidentiality, and the consequences of unauthorized disclosure.

- **Employee Training and Policies**: Regularly train employees on the importance of trade secrets and the procedures for maintaining confidentiality. Implement clear policies regarding the use, storage, and transmission of trade secrets, and require employees to acknowledge and agree to these policies in writing.

- **Access Controls**: Limit access to trade secrets to only those employees, contractors, or partners who need to know the information to perform their duties. Use physical security measures such as locks, security badges, and surveillance cameras, as well as digital controls like passwords, encryption, and access logs to prevent unauthorized access.
- **Physical and Digital Security**: Protect trade secrets stored in physical form (e.g., documents, prototypes) by using locked cabinets, secure storage rooms, and restricted areas. For digital information, use firewalls, encryption, secure servers, and regular backups to protect against hacking, data breaches, or accidental loss.
- **Exit Interviews and Post-Employment Clauses**: Conduct exit interviews with departing employees to remind them of their confidentiality obligations. Include clauses in employment agreements that prohibit former employees from using or disclosing trade secrets after they leave the company.
- **Regular Audits and Monitoring**: Regularly audit and monitor access to trade secrets to ensure compliance with security policies and detect any potential breaches or unauthorized disclosures. Promptly investigate any suspicious activities or potential security threats.
- **Documenting Protective Measures**: Maintain thorough records of all protective measures taken to safeguard trade secrets, such as signed NDAs, training sessions, access controls, and security audits. This documentation can serve as evidence in legal proceedings to demonstrate that reasonable efforts were made to maintain secrecy.

By implementing these protective measures, businesses can significantly reduce the risk of trade secret misappropriation and enhance their ability to enforce their rights in court if necessary. Maintaining a culture of confidentiality and vigilance is essential to ensuring that valuable trade secrets remain protected over time.

COMPARATIVE TAB

Type of Protection	Definition	Protected Elements	Duration of Protection	Key Requirements	Rights Granted	Legal Basis
Copyright	Protects original works of authorship fixed in a tangible medium.	Literary, musical, dramatic, artistic works, software, etc.	Life of the author + 70 years (or 95/120 years for works for hire or anonymous works).	Originality, fixation in a tangible medium.	Exclusive rights to reproduce, distribute, perform, display, and create derivative works.	Title 17 of the U.S. Code (Copyright Act of 1976).
Patent	Protects inventions that are new, useful, and non-obvious.	Utility patents: processes, machines, compositions of matter; Design patents: ornamental designs; Plant patents: new plant varieties.	Utility patents: 20 years from filing; Design patents: 15 years from grant; Plant patents: 20 years from filing.	Novelty, non-obviousness, usefulness, full disclosure.	Exclusive rights to make, use, sell, or import the patented invention or design.	Title 35 of the U.S. Code (Patent Act).
Trademark	Protects symbols, names, and slogans used to identify goods or services.	Words, phrases, logos, symbols, colors, sounds, etc.	Indefinite, as long as it is in use and renewal fees are paid.	Distinctiveness, use in commerce, non-generic.	Exclusive rights to use the mark and prevent others from using confusingly similar marks.	Lanham Act (15 U.S.C. §§ 1051 et seq.).
Industrial Design (Design Patent)	Protects the ornamental design of a functional item.	Ornamental aspects of articles of manufacture (e.g., product shapes, patterns).	15 years from the grant date.	Novelty, originality, ornamentality.	Exclusive rights to use, make, sell, or import the design.	Title 35 of the U.S. Code (35 U.S.C. § 171-173).

Trade Secret	Protects confidential business information that provides a competitive edge.	Formulas, recipes, business practices, processes, algorithms, etc.	Indefinite, as long as the secret is maintained.	Secrecy, economic value from not being known, reasonable measures to maintain secrecy.	Rights to prevent misappropriation, sue for damages, and obtain injunctions.	Defend Trade Secrets Act (DTSA) of 2016 (18 U.S.C. §§ 1836-1839).

1.2.1 Practical Questionnaire for Identifying Suitable Protection Types

The practical questionnaire is designed to help individuals and businesses determine the most appropriate type of intellectual property (IP) protection for their specific needs. By answering a series of targeted questions, users can identify which form of IP—such as copyright, patents, trademarks, design patents, or trade secrets—offers the most suitable protection for their creation, invention, or business strategy. This tool serves as a step-by-step guide to evaluating the nature, purpose, and commercial potential of their intellectual assets.

Purpose of the Questionnaire

The primary objective of the questionnaire is to provide a clear and systematic approach to identifying the correct form of IP protection. Since different types of IP protect different aspects of creations and inventions, choosing the wrong form of protection can lead to unnecessary costs, inadequate legal coverage, and lost opportunities. This questionnaire simplifies the decision-making process by addressing key factors that determine the most suitable type of IP.

Key Questions to Determine IP Type

The following questions are designed to help the user identify the most appropriate type of IP protection:

1. **What type of creation or invention do you have?**
   - Artistic work (e.g., painting, sculpture, music, literature, software code)
   - Invention or functional improvement (e.g., a new device, machine, process, chemical composition)

- Brand name, slogan, logo, or symbol (e.g., a business name, product name, tagline)
- Product design or ornamental feature (e.g., the shape of a bottle, the design of a piece of furniture)
- Confidential business information or processes (e.g., secret formula, marketing strategy, customer list)

2. **Is the creation tangible or intangible?**

- Tangible (e.g., a physical product, printed materials, digital files)
- Intangible (e.g., an idea, process, or method not yet fixed in a tangible form)

3. **Does the creation provide a competitive advantage, and if so, how?**

- Yes, through innovation or unique functionality (e.g., a new manufacturing process, innovative product)
- Yes, through brand recognition or market differentiation (e.g., a distinctive logo, brand name)
- Yes, through exclusive artistic or creative content (e.g., a novel, movie, software design)
- Yes, by maintaining secrecy (e.g., a recipe, algorithm, business strategy)
- No, it is a common or generic feature without a specific competitive edge.

4. **Is it essential to disclose the creation to the public, or is secrecy critical?**

- Disclosure is necessary to gain market access or build brand recognition (e.g., a new product launch, brand advertisement).
- Secrecy is critical to maintain a competitive edge (e.g., a secret formula, proprietary data).

5. **What is the intended commercial use of the creation?**

- Mass production or widespread commercial use (e.g., manufacturing a new product, selling software)

- Brand differentiation and marketing (e.g., establishing a brand, advertising services)
- Licensing or sale of rights (e.g., licensing an invention, selling a design)
- Exclusive use within the company (e.g., internal processes, confidential information)

Decision Tree and Scenarios

To provide clarity and assist in making a decision, the following decision tree visualizes the different pathways based on the answers to the above questions. It helps guide the user toward the most appropriate type of IP protection.

1. **Scenario A: Creation is an artistic work (e.g., literature, music, software code)**

   - If the work is original, fixed in a tangible medium, and meant for public dissemination:

     - **Recommended IP Protection: Copyright**

   - If the work includes a unique user interface or ornamental design that is visually distinct:

     - **Additional Protection: Design Patent**

2. **Scenario B: Invention or functional improvement (e.g., new device, process)**

   - If the invention is new, useful, and non-obvious and requires public disclosure:

     - **Recommended IP Protection: Utility Patent**

   - If the invention has unique ornamental aspects or aesthetics:

     - **Additional Protection: Design Patent**

3. **Scenario C: Brand name, slogan, logo, or symbol (e.g., business name, product name, tagline)**

   - If the brand element is distinctive and used in commerce to identify goods or services:

- ■ **Recommended IP Protection: Trademark**

4. **Scenario D: Product design or ornamental feature (e.g., unique packaging, product shape)**

   o If the design is new, original, and ornamental:

   - ■ **Recommended IP Protection: Design Patent**

   o If the design is also part of a brand identity:

   - ■ **Additional Protection: Trademark**

5. **Scenario E: Confidential business information or processes (e.g., trade secrets, proprietary algorithms)**

   o If the information provides a competitive advantage and is meant to be kept secret:

   - ■ **Recommended IP Protection: Trade Secret**

This decision tree can help clarify the appropriate IP protection by providing examples of typical scenarios and guiding the user based on their answers to the questionnaire.

1.2.2 Real-World Examples and Their IP Classifications

This section provides practical case studies that illustrate how different types of IP protection can be applied to various real-world situations. By analyzing these examples, readers can better understand the rationale behind selecting specific IP types and their respective benefits and limitations.

Case Study 1: Software Company Protecting Code and User Interface Design

- **Scenario**: A software company has developed a new software application with unique source code and a distinctive user interface (UI) design.

- **IP Protection Applied**:

   o **Copyright**: Protects the original software code, as it is considered a literary work fixed in a tangible medium. This prevents others from copying or distributing the software without authorization.

- o **Design Patent**: Protects the ornamental aspects of the user interface design if it meets the criteria for being new, original, and ornamental. This would prevent others from using a similar design that might confuse customers or diminish the company's brand identity.

- **Benefits**:

  - o **Copyright** provides broad protection for the software's functional and expressive elements.
  - o **Design Patent** offers additional protection for the unique visual elements of the software's interface, enhancing brand recognition.

- **Limitations**:

  - o **Copyright** does not protect the functional aspects or underlying concepts of the software.
  - o **Design Patent** only protects the specific visual design as depicted in the application drawings.

Case Study 2: New Product Design and Branding Strategy

- **Scenario**: A company has created a new product design with both functional and ornamental elements. It also wants to establish a strong brand identity using a distinctive name and logo.

- **IP Protection Applied**:

  - o **Utility Patent**: Protects the new and useful functional aspects of the product, such as its innovative features, methods of use, or manufacturing process.
  - o **Design Patent**: Protects the unique ornamental design of the product that distinguishes it from competitors.
  - o **Trademark**: Protects the product's brand name, logo, and any distinctive packaging used in commerce to differentiate the product.

- **Benefits**:
  - o **Utility Patent** provides a 20-year monopoly on the functional aspects of the product, preventing competitors from copying or using similar technology.
  - o **Design Patent** enhances product appeal by protecting the aesthetic elements for 15 years.
  - o **Trademark** ensures ongoing brand recognition and prevents others from using similar names or logos.

- **Limitations**:
  - o **Utility Patent** requires full public disclosure of the invention, potentially allowing competitors to design around the patented features.
  - o **Design Patent** only covers the specific ornamental design, not any functional aspects.
  - o **Trademark** protection requires continuous use and periodic renewal.

Case Study 3: Start-Up Developing a Unique Manufacturing Process

- **Scenario**: A start-up has developed a unique manufacturing process that provides a significant competitive advantage in terms of cost, speed, or quality.

- **IP Protection Applied**:
  - o **Trade Secret**: Protects the manufacturing process, keeping it confidential to maintain the competitive edge. The company uses NDAs with employees and partners, restricted access to information, and robust internal security measures.

- **Benefits**:
  - o **Trade Secret** protection can last indefinitely as long as the process remains secret, without the need for registration or public disclosure.
  - o Avoids the cost and time associated with patent applications.

- **Limitations**:
  - o If the secret is disclosed or reverse-engineered by others, the protection is lost.
  - o Trade secret protection does not prevent others from independently developing a similar process.

Case Study 4: Fashion Brand Protecting a Collection of Garments

- **Scenario**: A fashion brand has created a new collection of garments with unique patterns, designs, and a brand logo.

- **IP Protection Applied**:
  - o **Copyright**: Protects the original patterns and creative elements of the garment designs as artistic works.
  - o **Design Patent**: Protects the ornamental aspects of the garments if they meet the criteria for novelty and originality.
  - o **Trademark**: Protects the brand's logo, slogan, and any distinctive packaging used in commerce to differentiate the collection.

- **Benefits**:
  - o **Copyright** provides protection against unauthorized copying or reproduction of the designs.
  - o **Design Patent** offers additional protection for the aesthetic elements, preventing competitors from replicating the unique look.
  - o **Trademark** ensures brand recognition and differentiation in the market.

Key Takeaways from Each Case

These case studies highlight the strategic use of different types of IP protection to safeguard various forms of intellectual property. Here is an analysis of the reasoning behind each type of protection and the potential benefits and limitations:

1. **Combination of Copyright and Design Patents for Software Companies**
   - o **Reasoning**: Copyright is essential for protecting the software's underlying code, while a design patent provides additional protection for unique visual elements like a user interface that distinguishes the software from competitors.
   - o **Benefits**: Protects both functional and aesthetic aspects, ensuring broader coverage against infringement.
   - o **Limitations**: Copyright does not cover functional elements, and design patents may only protect the specific visual design as depicted.

2. **Comprehensive IP Strategy for New Products and Brands**
   - o **Reasoning**: A combination of utility patents, design patents, and trademarks ensures robust protection for a new product's functional, ornamental, and brand aspects. This approach prevents competitors from copying the product's technology, design, and branding.
   - o **Benefits**: Comprehensive protection covers all aspects of the product, enhancing market exclusivity and brand identity.
   - o **Limitations**: Requires substantial investment in filing and maintaining multiple IP rights and necessitates public disclosure of patented elements.

3. **Use of Trade Secrets for Proprietary Processes**
   - o **Reasoning**: Protecting a unique manufacturing process as a trade secret allows a start-up to maintain a competitive edge without disclosing proprietary information publicly.
   - o **Benefits**: Protection is potentially indefinite and avoids the costs and public disclosure associated with patenting.
   - o **Limitations**: Vulnerable to misappropriation, reverse engineering, and independent discovery, with no protection once secrecy is lost.

4. **Integrated IP Protection for Fashion Brands**

  o **Reasoning**: Using a combination of copyright, design patents, and trademarks protects the creative elements of garment designs, their ornamental aspects, and the brand identity.

  o **Benefits**: Protects multiple aspects of the fashion line, from design and aesthetics to brand recognition, creating a well-rounded IP strategy.

  o **Limitations**: Copyright may not provide global protection for fashion designs, and maintaining multiple IP rights can be costly.

These case studies also underscore the importance of a tailored IP approach that aligns with the specific characteristics, market goals, and legal requirements of each intellectual asset.

1.3 Assessment Checklist

This section provides a comprehensive checklist designed to help readers evaluate their intellectual property (IP) protection needs, ensuring all relevant aspects of IP law are covered. The checklist guides readers through identifying potentially protectable elements, assessing the value and risks associated with each type of IP, verifying legal requirements, and making informed decisions about their IP strategy.

1.3.1 Checklist for Evaluating IP Protection Needs

1. IP Inventory

Identify all potentially protectable elements of your business or project. This step ensures that you do not overlook any valuable IP assets. Consider the following:

- **Creative Works**:

  o Do you have any original written works, music, artwork, software, or audiovisual content?

  o Are there unique designs, patterns, or images used in your products or marketing?

  o Have you developed any manuals, guides, or training materials?

- **Inventions**:
  - Have you created any new products, devices, or machines?
  - Are there innovative methods, processes, or compositions you've developed?
  - Do you have new software algorithms or technologies?

- **Brand Elements**:
  - Have you created any distinctive names, logos, slogans, or symbols for your products or services?
  - Are there any distinctive colors, shapes, or packaging designs used in your branding?
  - Are there any sounds, scents, or other non-traditional trademarks associated with your brand?

- **Trade Secrets**:
  - Do you have any confidential business information, such as formulas, processes, customer lists, or marketing strategies?
  - Are there unique internal processes, data, or knowledge that provide a competitive edge?
  - Have you implemented measures to keep this information secret?

2. Evaluation Criteria

Evaluate each identified IP element based on key factors that influence its protection needs and potential benefits:

- **Commercial Value**:
  - How significant is the creation or invention to your business model?
  - Does it generate substantial revenue or have the potential to do so?
  - Is it critical to your competitive advantage in the marketplace?

- **Likelihood of Infringement**:
  - Is the IP easily replicable or likely to be copied by competitors?

- o Are there already similar products, designs, or brands in the market?
- o Is there a high likelihood of confusion or unauthorized use?

- **Importance of Exclusivity**:
  - o Would exclusive control over the IP strengthen your market position?
  - o Would licensing the IP to others create additional revenue streams?
  - o Is exclusivity essential to maintain brand identity and consumer trust?

- **Costs and Benefits of Protection**:
  - o What are the potential costs associated with filing for IP protection (e.g., application fees, legal costs)?
  - o What are the ongoing costs (e.g., renewal fees, monitoring for infringement, enforcement actions)?
  - o What are the potential financial and strategic benefits of obtaining protection?

3. Risk Assessment

Assess the risks associated with not protecting each type of IP:

- **Potential Loss of Market Share**:
  - o Could competitors use or replicate your IP to capture part of your market?
  - o Would failure to protect your IP allow others to offer similar products or services at lower prices?

- **Brand Dilution**:
  - o Could the use of a similar name, logo, or design by another entity dilute your brand's distinctiveness?
  - o Would unauthorized use of your IP weaken your brand's reputation or consumer trust?

- **Legal Disputes**:
  - o Are you at risk of being involved in costly legal disputes over ownership or infringement?
  - o Could your business face challenges proving ownership of the IP if it is not formally protected?

- **Impact on Innovation and Growth**:
  - o Could failing to protect your IP hinder your ability to innovate or attract investors?
  - o Would lack of protection limit your potential for expansion or partnerships?

5. **Legal Considerations**

Verify compliance with relevant U.S. IP laws and procedures:

- **Documentation**:
  - o Do you have proper documentation proving ownership and originality (e.g., dated drafts, records of development, contracts)?
  - o Are all agreements with employees, contractors, or partners regarding IP ownership in writing?

- **Registration Timelines**:
  - o Are you aware of the timelines for filing applications (e.g., deadlines for patent filings after public disclosure)?
  - o Have you considered international registration if you plan to expand into other markets?

- **Maintenance Requirements**:
  - o Are you aware of the renewal timelines and fees for maintaining your IP rights (e.g., trademarks, patents)?
  - o Have you established a system for tracking deadlines and ensuring timely renewals?

- **Enforcement Preparedness**:
  - o Have you developed a strategy for monitoring and enforcing your IP rights against potential infringers?

- o Are you prepared to take legal action if your IP is misused or infringed upon?

6. Decision Summary

Summarize your decisions regarding IP protection and outline the next steps:

- **Decide Which IP to Protect**:

  - o Based on the evaluation, determine which IP elements require formal protection (e.g., copyrights, patents, trademarks, trade secrets).
  - o Decide whether to file applications for multiple types of IP protection to cover different aspects of your creation or business.

- **Develop a Filing Strategy**:

  - o Prepare the necessary documents and information for filing IP applications (e.g., descriptions, drawings, claims).
  - o Identify the appropriate jurisdiction(s) for filing, considering domestic and international markets.

- **Draft Legal Agreements**:

  - o Create or update confidentiality agreements, employment contracts, and licensing agreements to secure IP rights and protect confidential information.
  - o Ensure all agreements align with your IP strategy and provide adequate legal safeguards.

- **Seek Professional Guidance**:

  - o Consult with IP attorneys or experts to navigate complex legal issues and maximize your IP protection.
  - o Consider engaging IP professionals for filing applications, drafting agreements, or handling enforcement actions.

By following this comprehensive checklist, businesses and creators can systematically evaluate their IP needs, identify potential risks and benefits, and develop a well-rounded strategy to protect and manage their intellectual property effectively.

Chapter 2:

Step-by-Step Guide to Filing and Registration in the United States

This chapter provides a detailed guide to the filing and registration procedures for various types of intellectual property (IP) in the United States. It explains the general steps, common requirements, and critical considerations that applicants must understand to navigate the U.S. IP system effectively. This section focuses on helping individuals and businesses prepare and submit their applications correctly to maximize their chances of successful registration.

General Filing Procedures

Overview of the U.S. Filing and Registration Process

The U.S. filing and registration process for intellectual property involves submitting an application to the relevant government agency, typically the United States Patent and Trademark Office (USPTO) or the U.S. Copyright Office, depending on the type of IP being protected. The process generally includes the following steps:

1. **Understanding the Type of IP Protection Needed**

   Before filing, applicants must determine the appropriate type of IP protection for their creation or invention. This involves assessing whether the IP qualifies as a patent, copyright, trademark, or trade secret. Each type of IP has specific eligibility criteria, and the choice will affect the application requirements, fees, and duration of protection.

2. **Preparing the Necessary Documentation**

   Applicants need to gather all relevant documentation required for the application. This typically includes:

   o **Detailed Descriptions**: A comprehensive description of the creation, invention, or brand element to be protected. For patents, this includes claims that define the scope of protection.

o **Drawings and Diagrams**: Visual representations of the invention or design, as necessary. Patent applications often require technical drawings, while trademark applications may include logos or packaging images.

o **Evidence of Use**: For trademarks, evidence of the mark's use in commerce (e.g., product labels, advertisements) may be required to establish the date of first use.

o **Disclosure Statements**: Any required statements, such as the "best mode" disclosure for patents, or statements of authorship and ownership for copyrights.

3. **Completing the Application Forms**

Applicants must accurately complete the specific application forms provided by the USPTO or the U.S. Copyright Office. Each form requires detailed information about the applicant, the creation, and the claimed IP rights. Common forms include:

o **Patent Applications**: Utility, design, or plant patent application forms, which include sections for descriptions, claims, and drawings.

o **Trademark Applications**: The Trademark Electronic Application System (TEAS) forms, such as TEAS Plus or TEAS Standard, which ask for information on the mark, goods/services, and owner.

o **Copyright Applications**: Forms for literary works, visual arts, performing arts, sound recordings, or software, with sections for title, authorship, and copyright claim.

4. **Submitting the Application**

Most IP applications in the U.S. are filed electronically:

o **Online Submission**: The USPTO and the U.S. Copyright Office provide electronic filing systems that guide applicants through the submission process. This method is faster, more efficient, and allows for immediate confirmation of receipt.

- o **Paper Submission**: Paper applications are also accepted but may incur additional fees and longer processing times.

5. **Paying the Applicable Fees**

   Filing fees vary depending on the type of IP and the specifics of the application (e.g., the number of claims in a patent, the type of trademark application). Applicants must ensure they pay the correct fees at the time of filing, as incomplete payments can delay or invalidate the application. Discounts may be available for small entities or micro-entities (individual inventors, small businesses, or non-profits).

6. **Awaiting Examination and Responding to Office Actions**

   After submission, the application undergoes examination by the relevant office:

   - o **Patent Examination**: Patent examiners review the application to determine whether the invention meets the criteria for patentability (novelty, non-obviousness, usefulness). This process may take several months to years.
   - o **Trademark Examination**: Trademark examiners evaluate the application for compliance with statutory requirements and check for potential conflicts with existing registered marks.
   - o **Copyright Examination**: Copyright applications are reviewed for proper documentation and compliance with registration requirements.

7. Examiners may issue "Office Actions," which are formal communications indicating issues with the application. Applicants must respond to these actions within a specified period, addressing the concerns raised and providing any additional information or amendments needed.

8. **Publication and Public Comment**

   For some types of IP, such as patents and trademarks, the application is published after a specific period to allow for public comment or opposition:

- **Patents**: Utility patent applications are typically published 18 months after filing, providing public notice of the invention.
- **Trademarks**: Trademarks are published in the USPTO's Official Gazette, allowing interested parties to file oppositions if they believe the mark conflicts with their own.

9. **Issuance or Registration**

If the examination is successful and any objections or oppositions are resolved, the IP is officially granted:

- **Patents**: A Notice of Allowance is issued, and the applicant must pay an issue fee to receive the patent grant.
- **Trademarks**: Once approved, the mark is registered, and a certificate of registration is issued.
- **Copyrights**: After approval, a certificate of registration is sent to the applicant.

10. **Maintaining IP Rights**

Post-registration, IP owners must take specific steps to maintain their rights:

- **Patents**: Maintenance fees must be paid at intervals (e.g., 3.5, 7.5, and 11.5 years for utility patents).
- **Trademarks**: Owners must file renewals and proof of use (e.g., Section 8 and Section 9 declarations) at required intervals.
- **Copyrights**: While there are no renewal fees, copyrights must be defended against infringement to maintain their full value.

Common Requirements and Steps

While each type of IP has unique requirements, several common elements apply across different types of IP applications:

1. **Clear and Accurate Descriptions**

All applications must provide clear, accurate, and comprehensive descriptions of the IP. For patents, this includes a detailed description of the invention, claims that define the scope of protection, and drawings that illustrate the invention. Trademark applications require a precise description of the mark and the goods/services it represents, while copyright applications need details about the nature of the work and authorship.

2. **Proof of Ownership and Entitlemen**

Applicants must establish that they have the legal right to apply for IP protection. This may involve providing:

- o **Proof of Authorship or Inventorship**: Documents proving that the applicant created the work or invention (e.g., contracts, employment agreements).
- o **Assignment Documents**: If the IP has been assigned or transferred, a written assignment document must be submitted.
- o **Statements of Use**: For trademarks, proof that the mark is being used in commerce in connection with the specified goods/services.

3. **Compliance with Formalities**

Applications must comply with specific formalities and legal requirements, including formatting, content, and submission procedures. Failure to adhere to these formalities can lead to delays or refusals:

- o **Patent Applications**: Must conform to formal requirements for format, length, and content, including margins, font size, and headings.
- o **Trademark Applications**: Must include all required information, such as the mark's description, the filing basis (use in commerce or intent to use), and a specimen showing how the mark is used.
- o **Copyright Applications**: Must include accurate information about the work, the authorship, and any disclaimers or limitations.

4. **Timely Responses to Communications**

Applicants must respond promptly to any communications or "Office Actions" from the USPTO or U.S. Copyright Office. Failure to respond within the specified deadlines can result in the abandonment of the application or a loss of rights. It is essential to monitor all correspondence carefully and provide timely and thorough responses.

5. **Understanding and Fulfilling Legal Requirements for Specific IP Types**

Each type of IP has unique legal requirements:

o **Patents**: Applicants must conduct prior art searches, draft detailed claims, and provide drawings. They must also disclose the best mode of practicing the invention and ensure that the application meets the standards for novelty and non-obviousness.

o **Trademarks**: Applicants need to ensure that the mark is distinctive, not generic or descriptive, and that it does not conflict with existing marks.

o **Copyrights**: Applicants must verify that the work qualifies as an original work of authorship and has been fixed in a tangible medium.

Copyright Registration Process

Copyright registration in the United States provides legal protection for original works of authorship, including literary, musical, artistic, and certain other intellectual works. While copyright protection is automatically granted upon the creation of a work, formal registration with the U.S. Copyright Office offers several legal advantages, including the ability to file infringement lawsuits and claim statutory damages.

Necessary Forms and Procedures for Copyright Registration in the U.S.

To register a copyright in the United States, the following steps and forms are typically required:

1. **Determine the Type of Work**

   The first step in the registration process is to identify the type of work you are registering. The U.S. Copyright Office categorizes works into various types, such as:

   o **Literary Works**: Books, articles, poetry, software code.
   o **Visual Arts**: Paintings, sculptures, drawings, graphic designs.
   o **Performing Arts**: Plays, choreography, films, and music.
   o **Sound Recordings**: Music recordings, audio books, podcasts.
   o **Motion Pictures/Audiovisual Works**: Movies, television shows, videos.
   o **Architectural Works**: Building designs, blueprints.

2. **Complete the Appropriate Application Form**

   Depending on the type of work, you will need to complete the relevant application form. The U.S. Copyright Office provides different forms for different types of works:

   o **Form TX**: For literary works, including software.
   o **Form VA**: For visual arts, including graphic designs and sculptures.
   o **Form PA**: For performing arts, including music, plays, and motion pictures.
   o **Form SR**: For sound recordings.
   o **Form SE**: For serials and periodicals.
   o **Form G/DN**: For group registration of daily newspapers and newsletters.

3. These forms can be filled out electronically through the U.S. Copyright Office's eCO (Electronic Copyright Office) system, or on paper if necessary.

4. **Prepare the Deposit Copy**

   The deposit copy is a copy of the work being registered, which must be submitted to the U.S. Copyright Office. The type of deposit required depends on the nature of the work:

- o **For Literary Works**: A complete copy of the manuscript or printed work.
- o **For Visual Arts**: High-quality photographs or digital images of the artwork.
- o **For Sound Recordings**: A copy of the recording and any associated material, such as liner notes or lyrics.
- o **For Motion Pictures**: A copy of the film, usually in a digital format.

5. The deposit must be submitted in a format that allows the Copyright Office to review and catalog the work effectively.

6. **Submit the Application and Pay the Fee**

Once the application form is completed and the deposit copy is prepared, the next step is to submit the application to the U.S. Copyright Office:

- o **Electronic Filing**: The most efficient method is to file electronically using the eCO system. This method is faster, more secure, and allows for quicker processing times.
- o **Paper Filing**: Applicants who prefer or are required to submit paper applications can mail the completed forms and deposit copies to the U.S. Copyright Office. However, this method is slower and may result in longer processing times.

7. The application must be accompanied by the appropriate filing fee, which varies depending on the type of work and the method of filing.

8. **Review and Approval**

After submission, the U.S. Copyright Office will review the application to ensure it meets all legal requirements. If the application is complete and accurate, the office will issue a certificate of registration. If there are issues with the application, the office may request additional information or corrections.

Costs, Processing Times, and Relevant Offices

1. **Costs**

   The fees for copyright registration depend on the type of work and the method of submission:

   - **Electronic Filing**: Generally less expensive, with fees ranging from $35 to $55 for standard applications.
   - **Paper Filing**: More costly, with fees typically around $125 for standard applications.
   - **Special Handling**: Expedited processing is available for an additional fee, which can be substantial, typically around $800, and is reserved for urgent cases (e.g., pending litigation or publication deadlines).

2. **Processing Times**

   Processing times can vary based on the type of work and the method of submission:

   - **Electronic Filing**: Generally faster, with processing times ranging from 3 to 6 months.
   - **Paper Filing**: Slower, often taking 9 to 12 months due to manual processing and mailing times.
   - **Expedited Processing**: If special handling is requested, processing can be completed in as little as 5 to 10 business days, depending on the urgency.

3. **Relevant Offices**

   All copyright applications in the U.S. are handled by the U.S. Copyright Office, located in Washington, D.C. The office provides various resources and support for applicants, including online tutorials, help desks, and customer service for inquiries related to the registration process.

By following these steps and understanding the associated costs and processing times, applicants can successfully navigate the copyright registration process, securing legal protection for their creative works.

Patent Filing Process

Filing a patent application in the United States is a complex process that requires careful preparation, adherence to legal standards, and thorough documentation. This section provides a detailed guide to the steps involved in submitting a U.S. patent application, the requirements for patentability, and tips for crafting a comprehensive patent application.

Steps for Submitting a U.S. Patent Application

1. **Determine the Type of Patent Needed**

   The first step is to determine which type of patent is appropriate for the invention:

   o **Utility Patent**: For new and useful processes, machines, articles of manufacture, or compositions of matter, or any new and useful improvement thereof.
   o **Design Patent**: For new, original, and ornamental designs for an article of manufacture.
   o **Plant Patent**: For new and distinct, invented or discovered, asexually reproduced plants.

2. **Conduct a Patent Search**

   Before filing, it is advisable to conduct a thorough patent search to identify any existing patents or published applications that may be similar to the invention. This helps to assess the novelty of the invention and avoid potential conflicts. The search can be conducted through:

   o **USPTO Patent Database**: The USPTO provides an online search tool where applicants can search for prior art.
   o **Professional Patent Search Services**: Hiring a patent attorney or search firm can provide a more comprehensive and detailed search, especially for complex inventions.

3. **Prepare the Patent Application**

   The patent application consists of several critical components, each of which must be prepared with precision:

- o **Specification**: A detailed written description of the invention, including how it works and how it is made and used. The specification should be clear enough to enable someone skilled in the field to replicate the invention.
- o **Claims**: The most critical part of the patent application, the claims define the legal boundaries of the invention. They must be drafted with care to cover the invention broadly enough to provide protection while avoiding prior art.
- o **Drawings**: If necessary, drawings must be included to illustrate the invention. These should be detailed and accurate, showing all aspects of the invention as claimed.
- o **Abstract**: A brief summary of the invention, highlighting its novel features and utility.
- o **Oath or Declaration**: The inventor must sign an oath or declaration attesting to the originality of the invention.

4. **File the Application with the USPTO**

The patent application is submitted to the USPTO, either electronically via the Electronic Filing System (EFS-Web) or by mail. Filing electronically is recommended for its efficiency and ease of tracking the application status. The submission must include the completed application forms, all required documents, and the applicable filing fees.

5. **Pay the Filing Fees**

Filing fees vary based on the type of patent, the complexity of the application, and the applicant's status (e.g., large entity, small entity, micro-entity). Applicants must pay the filing fee at the time of submission, along with any additional fees for excess claims, drawings, or expedited processing.

6. **Respond to USPTO Communications**

After filing, the USPTO will review the application. Examiners may issue an "Office Action," raising objections or rejections based on prior art or other issues. Applicants must respond to these communications within the specified time frame, providing arguments, amendments, or additional information as needed.

7. Publication of the Application

Typically, a utility patent application is published 18 months after the filing date, unless a non-publication request is made. This publication provides public notice of the pending application and allows others to submit prior art that may impact the patentability of the invention.

8. Issuance of the Patent

If the USPTO determines that the application meets all legal requirements and any objections are resolved, a Notice of Allowance is issued. The applicant must then pay the issue fee to have the patent granted and published in the Official Gazette. Once granted, the patent confers exclusive rights to the invention for the duration of the patent term.

Requirements for Novelty, Inventiveness, and Industrial Applicability

1. Novelty

The invention must be new, meaning it has not been publicly disclosed or known before the filing date. Any prior art that describes the invention or makes it obvious can disqualify it from patentability.

2. Inventiveness (Non-Obviousness)\

The invention must involve an inventive step, meaning it is not obvious to a person of ordinary skill in the relevant field at the time of the invention. This requires demonstrating that the invention represents a significant technological advancement or an unexpected result.

3. Industrial Applicability (Utility)

The invention must be capable of being used in some type of industry. This requirement is typically easy to satisfy, provided the invention has a specific, substantial, and credible utility.

Tips for Crafting a Comprehensive Patent Application

1. Use Clear and Precise Language

The language used in the application should be clear, precise, and specific. Avoid vague terms or ambiguous descriptions that could weaken the scope of the claims or lead to misunderstandings during examination.

2. Draft Strong Claims

Claims are the most critical part of a patent application. Draft them to be as broad as possible while still being specific enough to avoid known prior art. Consider including a mix of independent and dependent claims to provide layers of protection.

3. Include Detailed Drawings

High-quality drawings can significantly enhance the clarity of a patent application. Ensure that all elements of the invention are clearly depicted and that the drawings conform to USPTO standards.

4. Conduct a Thorough Prior Art Search

Performing a comprehensive search for prior art can help identify potential obstacles early and guide the drafting of claims that are more likely to be granted. It also prepares the applicant to address potential objections from the USPTO.

5. Consult with a Patent Attorney

Due to the complexity of patent law and the potential value of a patent, it is often advisable to consult with an experienced patent attorney. An attorney can help draft a robust application, respond to office actions effectively, and navigate the legal intricacies of the patent process.

Trademark and Design Registration Procedures (8-10 pages)

Trademarks and design patents are critical forms of IP that protect brand identity and product design. This section outlines the processes for registering trademarks and designs, detailing the necessary steps, specific requirements, and potential grounds for refusal.

Registration Steps for Trademarks and Designs

Trademark Registration Process

1. **Determine the Appropriate Filing Basis**

   The first step in the trademark registration process is to determine the appropriate filing basis for the application:

   o **Use in Commerce**: If the trademark is already in use in U.S. commerce, the applicant must provide evidence of this use, including the date of first use and a specimen showing how the mark is used in connection with the goods or services.

   o **Intent to Use**: If the trademark is not yet in use, but the applicant intends to use it in the future, they can file on an intent-to-use basis. This basis requires filing an additional "Statement of Use" once the mark is used in commerce.

2. **Conduct a Trademark Search**

   Before filing, it is highly recommended to conduct a comprehensive trademark search to ensure that the mark is not already in use or registered by another party. This search can be conducted using:

   o **USPTO Trademark Electronic Search System (TESS)**: The USPTO provides an online database where applicants can search for existing marks.

   o **Professional Trademark Search Services**: For a more thorough search, especially for common law uses not registered with the USPTO, consider using a professional search firm or attorney.

3. **Prepare the Application**

Applicants must prepare the trademark application, which includes the following key components:

- o **Applicant Information**: Name, address, and legal entity type (individual, corporation, LLC, etc.).
- o **Mark Information**: A clear representation of the mark (standard character, design, or composite). For design marks, a black-and-white or color image is required.
- o **Goods/Services Description**: A specific and accurate description of the goods or services associated with the mark, categorized according to the USPTO's Acceptable Identification of Goods and Services Manual.
- o **Filing Basis**: Indicate whether the mark is filed under "use in commerce" or "intent to use."
- o **Specimen of Use**: For use-based applications, a specimen demonstrating the mark's use in commerce (e.g., product labels, packaging, website screenshots).

4. **Submit the Application to the USPTO**

Applications are submitted to the USPTO through the **Trademark Electronic Application System (TEAS)**. Applicants can choose between:

- o **TEAS Plus**: Offers a reduced filing fee but requires stricter adherence to USPTO standards, including a complete and accurate identification of goods/services.
- o **TEAS Standard**: Allows more flexibility in describing goods/services but at a higher filing fee.

5. **Pay the Filing Fee**

Filing fees for trademarks depend on the application type (TEAS Plus or TEAS Standard) and the number of classes of goods or services covered. The fee must be paid at the time of submission to avoid delays.

6. **USPTO Examination**

   After submission, a USPTO trademark examiner reviews the application to determine if it meets all legal requirements:

   o **Substantive Examination**: The examiner checks for compliance with statutory requirements, including distinctiveness, proper classification of goods/services, and absence of conflicts with existing marks.
   o **Office Action**: If any issues are found, the examiner will issue an Office Action detailing objections or refusals. The applicant must respond within six months to address these concerns.

7. **Publication in the Official Gazette**

   If the application passes the examination, the mark is published in the **USPTO's Official Gazette** for a 30-day opposition period. During this time, third parties may oppose the registration if they believe the mark would cause confusion or dilute their own trademark.

8. **Issuance of Registration**

   If no opposition is filed, or if any opposition is successfully resolved, the USPTO issues a Certificate of Registration for marks filed on a use basis. For intent-to-use applications, the applicant must file a **Statement of Use** and receive a Notice of Allowance before registration.

9. **Maintain and Renew the Trademark**

   After registration, the trademark owner must file specific maintenance documents to keep the registration active:

   o **Section 8 Declaration**: Filed between the 5th and 6th year after registration to confirm the mark's continued use.
   o **Section 9 Renewal Application**: Filed every 10 years to renew the registration.
   o **Section 15 Declaration of Incontestability**: Optional filing after 5 years of continuous use, providing additional legal protection.

Design Patent Registration Process

1. **Determine Eligibility for Design Patent**

   The first step is to confirm that the design meets the criteria for design patent protection:

   o **New and Original**: The design must be new and original, meaning it has not been disclosed publicly before the filing date.

   o **Ornamental**: The design must be purely ornamental and not dictated by functional considerations.

2. **Prepare the Design Patent Application**

   The design patent application consists of several parts:

   o **Title**: A title that identifies the article to which the design applies.

   o **Description**: A brief description of the design, including any specific features that are critical to the design's uniqueness.

   o **Drawings or Photographs**: Detailed visual representations of the design, showing all perspectives (e.g., front, rear, side views). These must be clear and accurate, as they form the basis of the protection.

   o **Claim**: A single claim stating that the patent is for the ornamental design as shown in the provided drawings or photographs.

3. **Submit the Application to the USPTO**

   The design patent application can be submitted electronically via the **USPTO's EFS-Web system**. Ensure that all documents, including drawings, descriptions, and fees, are submitted correctly.

4. **Pay the Filing Fee**

   The filing fee for a design patent application varies depending on the applicant's status (large entity, small entity, or micro-entity). Ensure the correct fee is paid to avoid delays.

5. **USPTO Examination**

   A USPTO design patent examiner reviews the application to verify compliance with statutory requirements. This includes:

   o **Formal Examination**: Ensuring that the drawings and descriptions meet all formal requirements.

   o **Substantive Examination**: Determining that the design is new, original, and ornamental and does not conflict with prior art.

6. **Respond to Office Actions**

   If the examiner raises any issues or objections, the applicant must respond to the Office Action with amendments or arguments within the specified timeframe.

7. **Issuance of the Design Patent**

   If the application meets all requirements, the USPTO will issue a design patent. Design patents are not subject to maintenance fees and remain in force for 15 years from the grant date.

Specific Requirements and Grounds for Refusal

Trademark Registration Requirements and Grounds for Refusal

1. **Distinctiveness**

   Trademarks must be distinctive, meaning they are capable of identifying and distinguishing the source of goods or services. Marks are assessed along a spectrum:

   o **Fanciful or Arbitrary Marks**: Made-up or common words used in an unrelated context (e.g., "Xerox" for photocopiers).

   o **Suggestive Marks**: Hints at some quality or characteristic of the goods or services (e.g., "Netflix" for streaming services).

   o **Descriptive Marks**: Directly describe a characteristic or quality of the goods or services and generally require proof of secondary meaning to be registered (e.g., "Cold and Creamy" for ice cream).

- o **Generic Marks**: Common terms for the product or service itself and are never registrable (e.g., "Computer" for computers).

2. **Use in Commerce**

   For a mark to be registered, it must be used in commerce that Congress may regulate (interstate commerce, commerce between the U.S. and a foreign country, etc.). Applicants must provide a specimen demonstrating the mark's use.

3. **Grounds for Refusal**

   Several grounds can lead to refusal of a trademark registration:

   - o **Likelihood of Confusion**: The mark is confusingly similar to an existing registered mark or a pending application for similar goods/services.
   - o **Descriptiveness**: The mark is merely descriptive and lacks distinctiveness.
   - o **Geographic Descriptiveness**: The mark is primarily geographically descriptive (e.g., "California Wines").
   - o **Deceptiveness**: The mark is deceptive or misdescriptive regarding the nature, quality, or origin of the goods or services.
   - o **Scandalous or Immoral Marks**: The mark is considered offensive, scandalous, or immoral.

Design Patent Requirements and Grounds for Refusal

1. **New and Original**

   The design must be new and original, not previously disclosed in any prior art or publicly known. Prior art includes any similar designs publicly available before the filing date.

2. **Ornamentality**

   The design must be ornamental, meaning it must pertain to the appearance of the article rather than its functional features. Designs dictated purely by function cannot be patented.

3. **Non-Obviousness**

While the non-obviousness requirement for design patents is less stringent than for utility patents, the design must not be a trivial modification of an existing design that would be obvious to a designer of ordinary skill in the field.

4. **Grounds for Refusal**

    The USPTO may refuse a design patent application based on several grounds:

    o **Lack of Novelty**: The design is identical or substantially similar to an existing design in the public domain.
    o **Functional Design**: The design is primarily functional, not ornamental.
    o **Indefiniteness**: The drawings or photographs are unclear, incomplete, or do not provide a full disclosure of the design.
    o **Multiple Designs**: The application includes more than one design, which requires separate applications for each design.

Sample Forms and Templates

Completing the required forms correctly is a critical step in the IP registration process. This section provides examples of filled-out forms for each registration type—copyright, patent, trademark, and design patent—along with detailed guidelines for properly completing these documents to avoid common mistakes and delays.

Examples of Filled-Out Forms for Each Registration Type

1. Copyright Registration Form (eCO Online Application Example)

- **Application Type**: Literary Work (e.g., a novel or software code)

- **Form TX Example**:

    o **Title**: "The Adventures of Time Traveler"
    o **Author Information**:
        - Name: John Doe
        - Nationality: U.S. Citizen
        - Year of Birth: 1985
    o Work Made for Hire: No

- o Date of Creation: January 15, 2023
- o Nature of Authorship: Text
- o Rights and Permissions Contact: Jane Smith, ABC Publishing, contact@example.com
- o Deposit Copy: Full manuscript uploaded as a PDF file
- o Filing Fee: $55 for an electronic standard application

- **Notes**: Ensure that all sections are filled out accurately, especially the author's information and the nature of authorship. For joint authors, include details for each co-author.

2. Patent Application Form (Utility Patent Example - USPTO Form PTO/AIA/01)

- **Application Type**: Utility Patent for a new kitchen appliance (e.g., a multi-functional food processor)

- **Form PTO/AIA/01 Example**:

  - o **Title of Invention**: "Multi-Functional Food Processor with Auto-Cleaning Feature"
  - o **Inventor Information**:
    - Name: Emily Brown
    - Residence: 123 Main Street, Springfield, IL, 62704
    - Citizenship: U.S. Citizen
  - o **Correspondence Address**: Law Firm of XYZ, 456 Innovation Avenue, Chicago, IL, 60601
  - o **Application Type**: Non-Provisional
  - o **Claims**: 10 total claims (3 independent, 7 dependent)
  - o **Drawings**: 5 sheets of drawings illustrating the various features and functions
  - o **Filing Fee**: Calculated based on a small entity status ($400 for basic filing fee, plus $80 for each independent claim over three)

- **Notes**: Ensure that the specification is comprehensive, with clear and concise claims. The abstract should summarize the invention's novel features. Drawings must be in compliance with USPTO standards, showing all perspectives.

3. Trademark Registration Form (TEAS Plus Application Example)

- **Application Type**: Word Mark (e.g., "GreenLeaf Organics" for organic skincare products)

- **TEAS Plus Form Example**:
  - Applicant Information:
    - Name: GreenLeaf Organics, LLC
    - Address: 789 Market Street, San Francisco, CA, 94111
    - Entity Type: Limited Liability Company (LLC)
  - **Mark Information**: "GreenLeaf Organics" (Standard Character Mark)
  - **Goods/Services Description**: "Class 3: Organic skincare products, namely, lotions, creams, and facial cleansers."
  - **Filing Basis**: Section 1(a) - Use in Commerce
  - **Specimen**: Digital photograph of product packaging with the mark clearly visible
  - **Signature**: Signed by John Green, CEO
  - **Filing Fee**: $250 per class (TEAS Plus)

- **Notes**: Ensure the description of goods/services matches the Acceptable Identification of Goods and Services Manual. The specimen must clearly show the mark in use in commerce.

4. Design Patent Application Form (USPTO Form PTO/AIA/05)

- **Application Type**: Design Patent for a new chair design

- **Form PTO/AIA/05 Example**:
  - **Title of Design**: "Ornamental Design for a Chair"
  - **Inventor Information**:
    - Name: Mark Johnson
    - Residence: 321 Oak Lane, Miami, FL, 33101
    - Citizenship: U.S. Citizen
  - **Drawings or Photographs**: Six views (front, rear, left side, right side, top, bottom) showing the ornamental features of the chair.
  - **Description**: "The ornamental design for a chair, as shown and described."

- o **Claim**: "I claim the ornamental design for a chair as shown."
- o **Filing Fee**: $240 (micro-entity status)
- **Notes**: Ensure that all drawings are clear, well-defined, and accurately depict the design from all necessary angles. Only one claim is needed, as design patents are limited to a single claim.

Guidelines for Proper Completion of Documents

1. **Accuracy and Completeness**

   - o Ensure that all information provided on the forms is accurate and complete. Double-check names, addresses, and contact information to prevent correspondence delays.
   - o Review all required sections to ensure nothing is omitted. Missing information can lead to delays or refusal of the application.

2. **Consistent Use of Terms**

   - o Use consistent terminology throughout the application, particularly when describing the invention, design, or trademark. Avoid ambiguity and ensure that all terms are defined and used uniformly.

3. **Adherence to Formal Requirements**

   - o Follow specific formatting and layout requirements as dictated by the USPTO or U.S. Copyright Office:

     - ■ **Font and Margins**: Use standard fonts (e.g., Times New Roman, 12-point) and maintain adequate margins.
     - ■ **Spacing and Numbering**: Properly number pages and sections; use single or double spacing as required.
     - ■ **Headings and Subheadings**: Organize content with appropriate headings and subheadings to facilitate readability.

4. **Proper Use of Drawings and Specimens**

   - o **Drawings**: For patent applications, ensure that all drawings are detailed, labeled, and comply with USPTO standards. Use black ink on white paper, with no shading or color, unless color is essential to the invention.

- o **Specimens**: For trademark applications, provide clear, high-quality specimens that demonstrate the mark's use in commerce. Digital photos or screenshots should be in color if the mark includes color as a feature.

5. **Comply with Submission Guidelines**

- o When filing electronically, follow the submission guidelines on the USPTO or U.S. Copyright Office websites. Ensure that all forms are completed and uploaded correctly, and that the electronic payment process is finalized.
- o For paper filings, use appropriate mailing methods (e.g., certified mail) to ensure delivery and tracking.

6. **Include Correct Fees and Documentation**

- o Verify that the correct fees are calculated and included with the application. Fees vary depending on the type of application, the number of claims (for patents), or the number of classes (for trademarks).
- o Ensure all necessary supporting documents are included, such as drawings, declarations, or assignments, and that they are signed by the appropriate parties.

7. **Monitor Application Status**

- o After submission, regularly check the status of the application through the USPTO's Trademark Status and Document Retrieval (TSDR) system for trademarks or the Patent Application Information Retrieval (PAIR) system for patents. This helps ensure that any Office Actions or requests for additional information are addressed promptly.

8. **Respond to Office Actions Promptly**

- o If you receive an Office Action, review it carefully and respond within the specified timeframe (usually six months). Provide clear arguments, amendments, or additional documentation as needed to address the issues raised by the examiner.

By following these guidelines and using the sample forms as references, applicants can effectively complete and submit their IP registration documents, increasing their chances of a successful outcome. Properly completed forms and adherence to all requirements will help avoid common errors, reduce processing delays, and improve the likelihood of obtaining IP protection.

Chapter 3:
Classifying Work for Registration in the United States

This chapter explains the importance of proper classification when filing for intellectual property (IP) registration in the United States. It provides a detailed guide to classifying patents, trademarks, and designs according to the United States Patent and Trademark Office (USPTO) and International Patent Classification (IPC) systems. Accurate classification is essential for ensuring smooth processing of applications, facilitating searches, and establishing the scope of protection.

The Importance of Proper Classification

Proper classification is a critical component of the IP registration process in the United States. Correctly categorizing your work can significantly impact the outcome of your application, its legal protection, and the ease of enforcing your rights.

The Role of Classification in U.S. IP Registration

1. **Facilitating the Search Process**

   Classification systems are designed to organize IP into specific categories based on its nature and use. When filing a patent or trademark application, the proper classification of the work:

   o **Improves Searchability**: Accurate classification helps IP examiners and other stakeholders efficiently search and review prior art or existing marks. This is crucial for determining the novelty of an invention or the distinctiveness of a trademark.

   o **Minimizes Conflicts**: Proper classification reduces the likelihood of an application being rejected due to conflicts with existing IP rights. It ensures that the work is compared against the most relevant prior art or registered marks within the correct category.

2. **Ensuring Comprehensive Protection**

    Proper classification is essential for obtaining the full scope of protection for your IP:

    o   **Broad Coverage**: For patents, accurate classification ensures that the invention is fully covered within its intended field, protecting it from potential infringement.
    o   **Market Relevance**: For trademarks, correct classification ensures that the mark is registered in the appropriate classes of goods or services, reflecting its intended commercial use and safeguarding its market presence.

3. **Streamlining the Examination Process**

    Correct classification speeds up the examination process by ensuring that the application is reviewed by examiners with the appropriate expertise:

    o   **Specialized Examination**: Examiners are assigned based on their knowledge of specific classes. Proper classification ensures the application reaches the right examiner, reducing delays and increasing the likelihood of a favorable outcome.
    o   **Efficiency**: A well-classified application is less likely to encounter administrative hurdles, reducing the overall processing time.

4. **Legal and Strategic Considerations**

    Accurate classification has legal implications that affect the enforceability of IP rights:

    o   **Legal Clarity**: Proper classification helps avoid ambiguities regarding the scope of protection, making it easier to enforce IP rights in cases of infringement.
    o   **Strategic Filing**: Applicants can strategically classify their work to maximize protection or avoid conflicts with existing IP. For example, a broader classification may offer wider protection, while a narrower one may prevent conflicts.

Patent Classification Guide

Patents are classified according to established systems that categorize inventions based on their technical features. In the United States, two primary classification systems are used: the USPTO's classification system and the International Patent Classification (IPC) system.

Overview of USPTO and IPC Classification Systems

1. USPTO Classification System

The United States Patent and Trademark Office (USPTO) maintains a classification system that categorizes patents into various classes and subclasses:

- o **Classes**: Broad categories that group inventions based on their function or use. Each class represents a major technological area, such as "Class 29 - Metal Working" or "Class 705 - Data Processing."
- o **Subclasses**: Subdivisions within each class that further categorize inventions based on specific features, components, or methods. For example, within "Class 705 - Data Processing," there could be subclasses for "Financial Transactions," "Inventory Management," or "Cryptography."
- o **Purpose**: The USPTO classification system aids in the examination process by helping patent examiners locate relevant prior art. It is also useful for conducting searches to determine the novelty of an invention.

2. International Patent Classification (IPC) System

The International Patent Classification (IPC) system, managed by the World Intellectual Property Organization (WIPO), provides a standardized way to classify patents globally:

- o **Structure**: The IPC system divides patents into eight primary sections, each representing a broad area of technology (e.g., "A - Human Necessities," "B - Performing Operations, Transporting"). Each section is further divided into classes, subclasses, groups, and subgroups.

o **Hierarchy**: The IPC classification uses a hierarchical structure, with each level providing more specific details about the patent's technical content. For example, "A61" represents "Medical or Veterinary Science," while "A61B" refers to "Diagnosis; Surgery; Identification," and "A61B 5/00" covers "Measuring for Diagnostic Purposes."

o **Purpose**: The IPC system promotes uniformity in patent classification across different jurisdictions, making it easier to search for and compare patents internationally. It facilitates collaboration and information sharing between patent offices worldwide.

3. **Relationship Between USPTO and IPC Systems**

While the USPTO uses its classification system, it also adopts the IPC system to align with international practices:

o **Dual Classification**: Many U.S. patents are assigned both USPTO and IPC classifications to ensure they are searchable both domestically and internationally.

o **Cross-Referencing**: USPTO examiners often cross-reference IPC classifications when conducting prior art searches, ensuring comprehensive coverage of potential overlaps.

Examples of Commonly Classified Inventions

Understanding how inventions are classified can help applicants navigate the patent process more effectively. Here are some examples of commonly classified inventions:

1. **Medical Devices and Equipment**

o **USPTO Class 600 - Surgery**: This class includes various medical instruments and devices used in surgical procedures, such as scalpels, endoscopes, and suturing devices. Subclasses might cover specific types of instruments, like those designed for laparoscopic surgery or cardiac procedures.

- IPC Section A61 - Medical or Veterinary Science: Includes subclasses like "A61B - Diagnosis; Surgery; Identification," which covers inventions related to diagnostic tools, surgical instruments, and medical imaging devices.

2. **Computer Hardware and Software**

- **USPTO Class 345 - Computer Graphics Processing and Selective Visual Display Systems**: This class includes inventions related to graphical user interfaces (GUIs), computer graphics hardware, and display technologies. Subclasses could cover specific applications like virtual reality or augmented reality systems.
- **IPC Section G06 - Computing; Calculating; Counting**: This section includes inventions related to computers, data processing, and algorithms. For example, "G06F - Electrical Digital Data Processing" encompasses hardware and software for computers, including processors, storage devices, and software applications.

3. **Chemical Compounds and Pharmaceuticals**

- **USPTO Class 514 - Drug, Bio-Affecting and Body Treating Compositions**: Covers inventions related to pharmaceuticals, including new chemical compounds, formulations, and methods of treatment. Subclasses might cover specific types of drugs, such as antibiotics, antivirals, or cancer treatments.
- **IPC Section C07 - Organic Chemistry**: This section includes inventions related to chemical compounds and processes for their preparation. "C07D - Heterocyclic Compounds" would cover inventions involving specific chemical structures used in pharmaceutical drugs.

4. **Mechanical Devices and Machinery**

- **USPTO Class 123 - Internal-Combustion Engines**: Covers inventions related to engines that operate on internal combustion principles, including components like pistons, cylinders, and fuel injection systems. Subclasses might cover specific types of engines, such as diesel or rotary engines.

- o **IPC Section F02 - Combustion Engines**: Includes inventions related to different types of internal combustion engines, their parts, and methods for their operation.

5. **Consumer Electronics**

- o **USPTO Class 455 - Telecommunications**: This class includes inventions related to communication devices like smartphones, radios, and wireless networks. Subclasses may cover specific aspects like mobile communication protocols, signal processing methods, or antenna designs.
- o **IPC Section H04 - Electric Communication Technique**: Covers inventions related to communication technologies, such as "H04L - Transmission of Digital Information," which includes methods for data encryption, error correction, and data compression.

Trademark and Design Classification Guide (5-6 pages)

Proper classification is crucial when applying for trademarks and design patents. This section provides an overview of the classification systems used by the United States Patent and Trademark Office (USPTO) for trademarks and the Locarno Agreement classification for industrial designs.

Trademark Classification by the USPTO

1. **Overview of the Trademark Classification System**

The USPTO uses the **Nice Classification System** (established by the Nice Agreement) to categorize trademarks. This system divides goods and services into 45 distinct classes:

- o **Classes 1-34**: Cover various goods, such as chemicals (Class 1), pharmaceuticals (Class 5), clothing (Class 25), and electronics (Class 9).
- o **Classes 35-45**: Cover different services, such as advertising (Class 35), telecommunications (Class 38), legal services (Class 45), and education (Class 41).

2. **Purpose of Trademark Classification**

The classification system serves several purposes:

- ○ **Facilitating Examination**: Helps USPTO examiners assess potential conflicts with existing marks in the same or related classes.
- ○ **Defining the Scope of Protection**: Determines the range of goods or services covered by the trademark, which is essential for enforcing rights and avoiding infringement.
- ○ **Improving Searchability**: Makes it easier for applicants and the public to search for existing trademarks in similar categories, reducing the likelihood of conflicts and refusals.

3. **Application Process and Use of Classes**

When applying for a trademark, the applicant must:

- ○ **Select the Appropriate Class(es)**: Identify the specific class(es) that best describe the goods or services associated with the mark. An application can cover multiple classes if the mark is used or intended to be used across different categories.
- ○ **Describe the Goods/Services**: Provide a detailed description of the goods or services within each class, ensuring they align with the USPTO's Acceptable Identification of Goods and Services Manual.
- ○ **Pay Fees Per Class**: Filing fees are charged per class, so accurate classification helps control costs while ensuring comprehensive protection.

Design Classification under the Locarno Agreement

1. **Overview of the Locarno Classification System**

The Locarno Classification, administered by the World Intellectual Property Organization (WIPO), provides an international standard for classifying industrial designs. This system is used by many countries, including the United States, to categorize design patents:

- **Structure**: The Locarno Classification comprises 32 classes and numerous subclasses, each corresponding to a specific type of product. For example:
  - **Class 1**: Foodstuffs
  - **Class 2**: Articles of clothing and haberdashery
  - **Class 26**: Lighting apparatus
- **Purpose**: The Locarno Classification system helps ensure consistent classification across jurisdictions, facilitating international design protection and harmonizing examination standards.

2. **Purpose of Design Classification**

Proper classification under the Locarno system is essential for:

- **Facilitating Examination**: Ensures that design examiners can efficiently locate relevant prior art and assess the originality of the design.
- **Streamlining International Registration**: Makes it easier for applicants to seek protection in multiple countries by ensuring uniform classification.
- **Improving Search and Enforcement**: Enhances the ability to search for similar designs and enforce rights against potential infringers.

3. **Application Process and Use of Classes**

When applying for a design patent:

- **Identify the Relevant Locarno Class**: Determine the correct class and subclass that correspond to the design based on the product's function or appearance.
- **Describe the Design**: Provide a clear and detailed description of the design, including its unique ornamental features.
- **Ensure Accurate Representation**: Include accurate and high-quality drawings or photographs that correspond to the Locarno class selected.

3.4 Classification Reference Tools (4-5 pages)

To assist applicants in accurately classifying their IP, this section provides quick-reference tables and tools for determining the appropriate classification for trademarks and designs.

Quick-Reference Tables for Accurate Classification

1. **Trademark Classification Table**

   A simplified reference table that lists the Nice classes and provides examples of goods or services for each class:This table provides a quick overview to help applicants select the correct class for their trademarks.

Class	Description	Examples
1	Chemicals	Industrial chemicals, adhesives
3	Cosmetics and Cleaning Preparations	Soaps, perfumes, hair care products
9	Electrical and Scientific Apparatus	Computers, smartphones, software
25	Clothing	T-shirts, shoes, hats
35	Advertising and Business Services	Marketing, consulting, retail store services
41	Education and Entertainment Services	Schools, sports activities, publishing

44	Medical and Veterinary Services	Medical clinics, veterinary care

2. Design Classification Table (Locarno)

A simplified table showing key Locarno classes and examples:

Class	Description	Examples
2	Articles of Clothing and Haberdashery	Dresses, hats, gloves
9	Packages and Containers for the Transport or Handling of Goods	Bottles, boxes, bags
11	Articles of Adornment	Jewelry, watches, accessories
12	Means of Transport or Hoisting	Cars, bicycles, elevators
24	Medical and Laboratory Equipment	Surgical instruments, diagnostic devices
26	Lighting Apparatus	Lamps, chandeliers, streetlights

3.5 Case Studies in Classification (3-4 pages)

This section provides practical case studies that demonstrate the importance of accurate classification in IP registration, highlighting common pitfalls and best practices.

Case Study 1: Trademark Classification for a New Beverage Brand

- **Scenario**: A company is launching a new energy drink and needs to register its brand name and logo.

- **Classification Process**:

  - **Class 32**: The mark is classified under "Non-alcoholic beverages" for the energy drink itself.
  - **Class 35**: The company also offers related services like promotional events, so an additional classification in "Advertising and Business Services" is appropriate.

- **Outcome**: By selecting the correct classes, the company ensures comprehensive protection for both the product and associated services, reducing the risk of conflicts or opposition.

Case Study 2: Design Classification for a New Furniture Line

- **Scenario**: A designer has created a new line of modular office furniture and wants to protect the unique design.

- **Classification Process**:

  - **Class 6 (Locarno)**: The design is classified under "Furniture," specifically focusing on modular office setups.
  - **Supporting Materials**: Detailed drawings are submitted, showing all aspects of the furniture's design, including joinery details, configurations, and unique aesthetic elements.

- **Outcome**: Accurate classification under the Locarno system ensures that the design is properly protected and facilitates international registration, providing a broader market reach.

Chapter 4:

Handling Confidential Information in the United States

This chapter explores the management and protection of confidential information in the United States, focusing on trade secrets. It provides an in-depth understanding of what constitutes a trade secret, the importance of protecting such information, and the legal framework governing trade secrets under the Defend Trade Secrets Act (DTSA) of 2016. This section also discusses practical strategies for maintaining confidentiality and responding to breaches.

4.1 Understanding and Importance of Confidential Information

Confidential information plays a crucial role in maintaining a competitive edge in the marketplace. Protecting such information is vital for businesses to safeguard their unique advantages, maintain customer trust, and avoid financial losses. The primary legal mechanism for protecting confidential business information in the United States is through trade secret law.

Explanation of Trade Secrets under the Defend Trade Secrets Act (DTSA)

1. **Definition of Trade Secrets**

   Under the Defend Trade Secrets Act (DTSA) of 2016, a trade secret is defined as all forms and types of financial, business, scientific, technical, economic, or engineering information, including formulas, patterns, compilations, programs, devices, methods, techniques, processes, or codes, whether tangible or intangible, and regardless of how stored or maintained, provided that:

   o The owner has taken reasonable measures to keep such information secret.

- The information derives independent economic value from not being generally known to, and not being readily ascertainable through proper means by, another person who can obtain economic value from its disclosure or use.

2. This broad definition covers a wide range of proprietary information, from manufacturing processes and product designs to marketing strategies, customer lists, and software algorithms.

3. **Key Elements of a Trade Secret**

   For information to qualify as a trade secret under the DTSA, it must meet the following criteria:

   - **Secrecy**: The information must not be generally known or readily accessible to others who can benefit economically from its disclosure or use. This means that the information should be known only to those within the company or organization who need to know it for their work.
   - **Economic Value**: The information must provide a competitive advantage because it is kept secret. If the information were to become public knowledge, it would lose its value to the owner. For example, a secret recipe for a popular beverage has economic value as long as it remains unknown to competitors.
   - **Reasonable Measures to Protect Secrecy**: The owner of the information must take reasonable steps to maintain its confidentiality. These measures can include physical security (e.g., locked rooms), digital security (e.g., encryption, access controls), legal agreements (e.g., non-disclosure agreements or NDAs), and internal policies (e.g., employee training and confidentiality clauses).

4. **Legal Basis and Scope of the Defend Trade Secrets Act (DTSA)**

   The DTSA was enacted in 2016 to provide a federal framework for trade secret protection, complementing existing state laws that follow the Uniform Trade Secrets Act (UTSA). The DTSA aims to create a consistent legal standard across the United States and offers several key features:

- **Federal Civil Cause of Action**: The DTSA allows trade secret owners to bring civil lawsuits in federal court against individuals or entities accused of misappropriating trade secrets. Before the DTSA, trade secret cases were generally limited to state courts, creating potential inconsistencies in rulings and enforcement.
- **Definition of Misappropriation**: Misappropriation under the DTSA includes acquiring a trade secret by improper means, such as theft, bribery, misrepresentation, breach of a duty to maintain secrecy, or espionage. It also covers the unauthorized disclosure or use of a trade secret by someone who knows or should know that the trade secret was acquired improperly.
- **Remedies and Damages**: The DTSA provides a range of remedies for trade secret owners, including:
  - **Injunctive Relief**: Court orders preventing the misappropriator from using or disclosing the trade secret.
  - **Monetary Damages**: Compensation for actual losses caused by the misappropriation, including damages for unjust enrichment or a reasonable royalty for unauthorized use.
  - **Exemplary Damages**: In cases of willful and malicious misappropriation, courts may award exemplary damages of up to twice the amount of actual damages.
  - **Attorney's Fees**: In certain cases, such as willful misappropriation or bad faith litigation, the prevailing party may be awarded reasonable attorney's fees.
- **Civil Seizure Provision**: A unique feature of the DTSA is the civil seizure provision, which allows a court to order the seizure of property to prevent the dissemination of trade secrets in extraordinary circumstances. This provision is designed to prevent the destruction, hiding, or transfer of trade secrets that could cause irreparable harm.

5. **Importance of Protecting Trade Secrets**

   Protecting trade secrets is crucial for several reasons:

   o **Maintaining Competitive Advantage**: Trade secrets often represent a company's most valuable assets, such as proprietary technology, confidential business information, or customer data. Protecting these assets helps maintain a competitive edge in the market.

   o **Safeguarding Innovation**: Innovation is a key driver of growth and profitability. By protecting trade secrets, businesses can ensure that their investments in research and development yield long-term benefits.

   o **Avoiding Financial Losses**: The loss or theft of trade secrets can result in significant financial damages, including lost revenue, reduced market share, and increased competition. It can also lead to legal disputes and reputational damage.

   o **Legal Enforcement and Deterrence**: A strong trade secret protection program, coupled with the legal tools provided by the DTSA, serves as a deterrent against misappropriation and enables businesses to take swift action against infringers.

6. **How to Qualify for Protection Under the DTSA**

   To qualify for protection under the DTSA, companies must:

   o **Take Reasonable Steps to Protect Confidential Information**: The DTSA requires that trade secret owners demonstrate they have taken reasonable measures to maintain the secrecy of their information. This can involve implementing physical, digital, and administrative safeguards, such as secure access controls, data encryption, and employee confidentiality agreements.

   o **Implement a Trade Secret Protection Policy**: Establish clear policies and procedures for identifying, managing, and protecting trade secrets. This can include training employees on the importance of confidentiality, marking documents as "confidential," and regularly reviewing and updating security measures.

- o **Ensure Legal Compliance**: Comply with relevant laws and regulations regarding data privacy, cybersecurity, and IP protection. This includes monitoring and enforcing NDAs, non-compete clauses, and other contractual obligations related to trade secrets.

Creating Effective Non-Disclosure Agreements (NDAs)

Non-Disclosure Agreements (NDAs) are legally binding contracts used to protect confidential information from unauthorized disclosure. They are crucial for businesses that wish to safeguard their trade secrets, proprietary information, and other sensitive data. This section outlines the steps for drafting a legally sound NDA in the U.S., along with key clauses and practical advice for creating an effective agreement.

Steps to Draft a Legally Sound NDA in the U.S.

1. **Determine the Type of NDA Required**

   Before drafting, identify the appropriate type of NDA based on the context of the relationship and the nature of the information to be protected. The two primary types of NDAs are:

   - o **Unilateral NDA**: Used when only one party is disclosing confidential information to the other. Commonly used when hiring employees, engaging contractors, or negotiating with potential partners.
   - o **Mutual NDA**: Used when both parties will be sharing confidential information with each other. Commonly used in joint ventures, partnerships, or mergers and acquisitions where both sides disclose sensitive information.

2. **Identify the Parties Involved**

   Clearly define all parties to the NDA, specifying their full legal names, addresses, and business structures (e.g., corporation, LLC, individual). This ensures that the agreement is binding and enforceable against all parties involved.

3. **Define the Purpose of the NDA**

   State the specific purpose for which the confidential information is being shared. This may include evaluating a potential business relationship, negotiating a contract, or developing a new product. Defining the purpose helps to limit the scope of disclosure and provides context for the agreement's enforceability.

4. **Clearly Define Confidential Information**

   Include a precise definition of what constitutes "Confidential Information." This can be done in several ways:

   o **Broad Definition**: Define confidential information broadly to cover all types of data, including financial data, business plans, technical information, customer lists, trade secrets, and proprietary technology.
   o **Specific Definition**: List specific categories or types of information considered confidential, such as "software code," "marketing strategies," or "product specifications."
   o **Exclusions**: Clearly state any information not considered confidential, such as information already in the public domain, information known to the receiving party before disclosure, or information obtained from a third party without breach of an NDA.

5. **Set the Duration of Confidentiality Obligations**

   Specify how long the confidentiality obligations will remain in effect. This could be:

   o **Fixed Term**: A specific number of years (e.g., 2, 5, or 10 years) after the termination of the NDA or completion of the purpose.
   o **Indefinite Term**: Until the confidential information is no longer considered a trade secret or loses its value due to public disclosure. The duration should balance the need for protection with the practical realities of maintaining secrecy over time.

6. **Outline the Obligations of the Receiving Party**

Clearly state the receiving party's obligations concerning the use and protection of the confidential information:

o **Non-Disclosure**: The receiving party must agree not to disclose the confidential information to third parties without the discloser's prior written consent.

o **Restricted Use**: The receiving party must agree to use the confidential information only for the specified purpose stated in the NDA.

o **Security Measures**: The receiving party must implement reasonable security measures to prevent unauthorized access, such as encryption, password protection, and restricted access.

7. **Include Clauses for Return or Destruction of Information**

Provide terms for the return or destruction of confidential information upon termination of the NDA or completion of the intended purpose:

o **Return of Information**: Require the receiving party to return all physical and digital copies of the confidential information.

o **Destruction of Information**: Alternatively, require the receiving party to destroy all copies of the information and certify in writing that this has been done. These provisions help ensure that the confidential information does not remain in the possession of the receiving party after the relationship ends.

8. **Specify Remedies for Breach of the NDA**

Include a clause outlining the remedies available to the disclosing party in case of a breach:

o **Injunctive Relief**: State that the disclosing party is entitled to seek an injunction to prevent further unauthorized use or disclosure.

- o **Monetary Damages**: Provide for the recovery of damages caused by the breach, including any lost profits, reputational harm, or costs incurred to mitigate the damage.
- o **Attorney's Fees**: Consider including a provision for the payment of attorney's fees and legal costs by the breaching party.

9. **Ensure Compliance with Applicable Law**

Specify the governing law and jurisdiction for any disputes arising under the NDA. Typically, the governing law is that of the state where the disclosing party is located. This ensures clarity on which laws will apply in case of a breach and where any legal proceedings will take place.

10. **Have the NDA Reviewed by Legal Counsel**

Given the legal complexities and potential consequences of NDAs, it is advisable to have the agreement reviewed by an attorney experienced in IP or contract law. This helps ensure that the NDA is legally sound, enforceable, and tailored to the specific needs of the parties involved.

Key Clauses and Practical Advice for Drafting

1. **Definition of Confidential Information Clause**

This clause defines what constitutes confidential information. A well-drafted clause should:

- o Include a broad definition to cover all potential types of sensitive information.
- o Specify any exclusions to clarify what is not covered.
- o Provide examples to help illustrate the scope of confidentiality.

2. **Obligations of the Receiving Party Clause**

This clause outlines the receiving party's responsibilities for maintaining confidentiality:

- o **Non-Disclosure**: The receiving party agrees not to disclose the information to unauthorized parties.

- o **Restricted Use**: The receiving party agrees to use the information solely for the intended purpose.
- o **Security Measures**: The receiving party agrees to implement adequate security measures to protect the information.

3. **Exceptions to Confidentiality Clause**

This clause lists circumstances where confidentiality obligations do not apply:

- o Information that becomes public knowledge through no fault of the receiving party.
- o Information that was already in the possession of the receiving party before disclosure.
- o Information obtained independently from a third party without a breach of any obligation.
- o Information required to be disclosed by law or court order (with notice to the disclosing party).

4. **Term and Termination Clause**

This clause specifies the duration of the NDA and the conditions under which it may be terminated:

- o **Fixed Term**: State the number of years the NDA will remain in effect.
- o **Event-Based Termination**: Specify conditions that terminate the NDA (e.g., completion of the project).
- o **Survival Clause**: Certain obligations, such as confidentiality, may survive termination for a specified period or indefinitely.

5. **Return or Destruction of Information Clause**

This clause requires the receiving party to return or destroy all copies of the confidential information at the end of the agreement:

- o Specify the timeframe for returning or destroying the information.
- o Require certification of destruction to confirm compliance.

6. **Remedies Clause**

This clause outlines the remedies available in case of a breach:

o **Injunctive Relief**: States that the disclosing party can seek a court order to prevent further breaches.
o **Monetary Damages**: Allows the disclosing party to seek financial compensation for any damages incurred.
o **Liquidated Damages**: Optional clause specifying a predetermined amount to be paid in case of a breach.

7. **Governing Law and Jurisdiction Clause**

This clause determines which state's laws will govern the NDA and the venue for any legal proceedings:

o Specify the state laws that apply to the agreement.
o Identify the appropriate court or jurisdiction for resolving disputes.

8. **Entire Agreement Clause**

This clause states that the NDA constitutes the entire agreement between the parties regarding the subject matter and supersedes any prior agreements or understandings:

o Helps avoid misunderstandings and disputes by ensuring that all terms are contained within the NDA.

9. **Severability Clause**

This clause ensures that if any part of the NDA is found to be invalid or unenforceable, the remainder of the agreement remains in effect:

o Provides flexibility and ensures that the NDA remains enforceable even if one provision is struck down.

10. **Signatures of All Parties**

Ensure that all parties sign the NDA, including representatives with the authority to bind their respective organizations legally. Electronic signatures may also be valid, depending on applicable state laws.

Protecting Confidential Information

This section discusses strategies for effectively safeguarding trade secrets in the United States. Given the importance of maintaining the confidentiality of trade secrets, businesses must adopt a multi-layered approach that includes legal, administrative, and technical measures. These strategies are critical to ensuring that trade secrets remain protected, both internally and externally, from unauthorized disclosure or misappropriation.

Strategies for Safeguarding Trade Secrets in a U.S. Context

Protecting trade secrets involves creating a robust framework that integrates various security measures and protocols. The following strategies are designed to help businesses maintain the secrecy of their valuable information:

1. **Implement Internal Confidentiality Policies and Procedures**
   Establishing clear internal policies and procedures is a foundational step in safeguarding trade secrets. These policies should cover the following aspects:

   o **Employee Training**: Regularly train employees on the importance of trade secret protection, emphasizing their role in maintaining confidentiality. Training should cover what constitutes a trade secret, the consequences of unauthorized disclosure, and best practices for handling confidential information.

   o **Access Control Policies**: Restrict access to trade secrets and confidential information only to employees who need it to perform their duties. Implement a "need-to-know" policy, where access is granted based on an employee's job function and level of responsibility.

   o **Confidentiality Agreements**: Require all employees, contractors, and third-party partners to sign confidentiality agreements (NDAs) as a condition of employment or engagement. Ensure that these agreements clearly outline the obligations of confidentiality and the consequences of breaches.

○ **Clear Labeling of Confidential Information**: Clearly label all documents, files, and materials containing trade secrets as "Confidential," "Proprietary," or "Trade Secret." This helps employees and third parties recognize the sensitive nature of the information and take appropriate precautions.

2. **Adopt Technical and Physical Security Measures**

Technical and physical security measures are essential to preventing unauthorized access to trade secrets. These measures should include:

○ **Digital Security**: Implement robust cybersecurity protocols to protect electronic data, such as:
  - **Encryption**: Use strong encryption methods to protect sensitive data at rest (stored data) and in transit (data being transferred across networks). Encryption ensures that even if data is intercepted, it cannot be easily read or used.
  - **Firewalls and Intrusion Detection Systems**: Use firewalls to create a barrier between internal networks and external threats, and deploy intrusion detection systems (IDS) to monitor and respond to suspicious activities in real-time.
  - **Access Controls**: Use role-based access controls (RBAC) to limit access to confidential information based on job roles. Implement multi-factor authentication (MFA) for accessing sensitive systems and data.
  - **Regular Security Audits and Penetration Testing**: Conduct regular security audits and penetration testing to identify and address vulnerabilities in your digital infrastructure.
○ **Physical Security**: Ensure that physical premises where trade secrets are stored are secure:
  - **Secure Storage**: Use locked cabinets, safes, or secure rooms to store physical documents and materials containing trade secrets.

- **Access Controls**: Implement access controls, such as key cards, biometric scanners, or security codes, to restrict entry to areas where confidential information is stored.
- **Surveillance and Monitoring**: Install surveillance cameras and monitoring systems to deter unauthorized access and monitor who enters and exits sensitive areas.

3. **Create a Culture of Confidentiality**

Building a culture that values and prioritizes confidentiality is crucial for protecting trade secrets. This involves:

o **Leadership Commitment**: Senior management should lead by example and emphasize the importance of protecting confidential information. Regular communications from leadership about the value of trade secrets and the consequences of breaches reinforce the message.

o **Regular Reinforcement**: Conduct regular training sessions, workshops, and awareness campaigns to reinforce the importance of confidentiality. Use real-world examples and case studies to demonstrate the risks and consequences of failing to protect trade secrets.

o **Confidentiality as a Core Value**: Embed confidentiality as a core value in the company's mission and ethics statements. Encourage employees to report any suspicious behavior or potential breaches and provide a clear reporting mechanism.

4. **Monitor and Audit Access to Trade Secrets**

Regular monitoring and auditing are essential to ensure that access to trade secrets is properly managed and controlled:

o **Access Logs and Monitoring**: Maintain detailed logs of who accesses confidential information and when. Regularly review these logs to identify any unusual or unauthorized access attempts.

o **Audit Trails**: Implement audit trails that track changes, downloads, and transfers of confidential information. This can help detect and respond to potential breaches quickly.

- o **Periodic Reviews**: Conduct periodic reviews of access permissions to ensure they align with current roles and responsibilities. Revoke access immediately when an employee changes roles or leaves the organization.

5. **Establish Strong Relationships with Third Parties**

Trade secrets are often shared with third parties, such as suppliers, contractors, and partners. To protect trade secrets in these relationships:

- o **Use Non-Disclosure Agreements (NDAs)**: Require all third parties who receive confidential information to sign NDAs that specify their obligations to protect the information and the consequences of breaches.
- o **Limit Information Sharing**: Share only the minimum amount of information necessary for the third party to perform its duties. Use confidentiality agreements to restrict the use of the information to the intended purpose only.
- o **Conduct Due Diligence**: Perform due diligence on potential partners, vendors, and contractors to assess their trustworthiness, security practices, and history of handling confidential information.
- o **Include Protective Clauses in Contracts**: Include clauses in contracts with third parties that mandate specific security measures for handling confidential information, audit rights, and penalties for breaches.

6. **Develop a Response Plan for Potential Breaches**

Even with robust measures in place, breaches can still occur. Developing a response plan is critical to mitigate damage:

- o **Incident Response Team**: Establish an incident response team that includes members from legal, IT, HR, and senior management. This team is responsible for handling potential breaches and coordinating response efforts.
- o **Immediate Actions**: Define immediate actions to be taken in case of a suspected breach, such as isolating affected systems, securing evidence, and notifying relevant stakeholders.

- o **Internal Investigations**: Conduct thorough internal investigations to determine the cause and extent of the breach. Work with law enforcement and forensic experts if necessary.
- o **Legal Remedies**: Be prepared to pursue legal remedies under the Defend Trade Secrets Act (DTSA) or state trade secret laws, such as seeking injunctions, monetary damages, and recovery of legal costs.

7. **Regularly Review and Update Protection Measures**

The landscape of cybersecurity and information protection is constantly evolving. Regularly review and update your protection measures to stay ahead of potential threats:

- o **Continuous Improvement**: Continuously evaluate the effectiveness of your security measures and make improvements as needed. Keep abreast of new technologies and best practices for trade secret protection.
- o **Review Legal Compliance**: Ensure that your protection strategies comply with all relevant laws and regulations. This includes federal laws, such as the DTSA, as well as state-level trade secret laws.
- o **Adapt to Changes**: Be prepared to adapt your strategies in response to changes in business operations, market conditions, or emerging threats. Regularly assess your risk exposure and make adjustments as necessary.

Managing Breaches of Confidentiality

When a breach of confidentiality occurs, it is essential for a business to act swiftly and strategically to contain the damage, mitigate risks, and enforce its rights. This section outlines the immediate actions that should be taken and the legal remedies available under U.S. law to address breaches of confidentiality.

Immediate Actions and Legal Remedies for Confidentiality Breaches

Immediate Actions Following a Breach

1. **Activate the Incident Response Plan**

   The first step in managing a breach of confidentiality is to activate the company's pre-established incident response plan. This plan should detail the procedures and protocols for responding to a breach, including:

   o **Assemble the Incident Response Team**: Bring together the designated incident response team, which should include members from key departments such as IT, legal, HR, public relations, and senior management.

   o **Assign Roles and Responsibilities**: Clearly define roles and responsibilities within the team to ensure a coordinated and efficient response. This may include designating team members to handle communication, technical analysis, and legal actions.

2. **Contain the Breach**

   It is crucial to contain the breach as quickly as possible to prevent further unauthorized access or dissemination of confidential information:

   o **Isolate Affected Systems**: Immediately isolate any compromised systems, networks, or databases to prevent further access or data exfiltration. This may involve disconnecting from the internet, shutting down affected servers, or disabling user accounts.

   o **Secure Physical Premises**: If the breach involves physical access (e.g., stolen documents or devices), secure the premises and restrict entry to areas where confidential information is stored.

   o **Preserve Evidence**: Preserve all evidence related to the breach, including digital logs, access records, and physical documents. This evidence will be critical for internal investigations and potential legal proceedings.

3. **Conduct an Internal Investigation**

An internal investigation should be launched immediately to determine the cause, scope, and impact of the breach:

o **Identify the Source**: Determine the origin of the breach and identify the individuals or entities responsible. This may involve analyzing access logs, interviewing employees, and reviewing surveillance footage.

o **Assess the Extent of the Damage**: Evaluate the extent of the breach, including the types of information compromised, the volume of data affected, and the potential impact on the business.

o **Document Findings**: Maintain detailed records of all findings, actions taken, and communications during the investigation. This documentation will be essential for any legal actions and compliance requirements.

4. **Notify Affected Parties**

Depending on the nature and scope of the breach, it may be necessary to notify affected parties, including:

o **Internal Stakeholders**: Inform senior management, board members, and other relevant personnel about the breach and the steps being taken to address it.

o **Customers and Partners**: If customer or partner information is compromised, notify them promptly and provide guidance on how to protect themselves from potential harm (e.g., changing passwords, monitoring accounts).

o **Regulatory Authorities**: In some cases, businesses are legally required to report breaches to regulatory authorities, such as the Federal Trade Commission (FTC) or state attorneys general, especially if the breach involves personally identifiable information (PII).

5. **Communicate Transparently**

Communication is key to managing a breach effectively and maintaining trust with stakeholders:

o **Internal Communication**: Keep employees informed about the breach and the actions being taken to address it. Provide clear instructions on any additional security measures or protocols they must follow.

o **External Communication**: Develop a public relations strategy to manage external communications, including press releases, social media statements, and customer notifications. Be transparent about the breach, its impact, and the steps being taken to prevent future incidents.

6. **Enhance Security Measures**

After a breach, it is essential to review and strengthen security measures to prevent future incidents:

o **Update Security Protocols**: Review existing security protocols and implement any necessary updates or improvements, such as enhancing encryption standards, changing access controls, or increasing monitoring capabilities.

o **Conduct Training**: Provide additional training for employees on recognizing and responding to security threats, protecting confidential information, and adhering to company policies.

o **Monitor Systems**: Increase monitoring of systems and networks for any signs of suspicious activity or additional breaches.

Legal Remedies for Confidentiality Breaches

1. **Seek Injunctive Relief**

Injunctive relief is a legal remedy that seeks to prevent further harm by stopping the unauthorized use or disclosure of confidential information. The following types of injunctive relief may be pursued:

- **Temporary Restraining Order (TRO)**: A TRO is a short-term court order that immediately prohibits the breaching party from using or disclosing the confidential information. It is typically issued to prevent imminent harm and is valid for a limited time until a more comprehensive hearing can take place.
- **Preliminary Injunction**: A preliminary injunction is a court order that extends the prohibition of the unauthorized use or disclosure of confidential information until the case is resolved. It requires a higher burden of proof than a TRO and usually involves a court hearing to determine its necessity.
- **Permanent Injunction**: A permanent injunction is a long-term court order that prohibits the breaching party from using or disclosing confidential information indefinitely. It is granted after a final ruling in favor of the plaintiff, usually at the conclusion of the trial.

2. **Pursue Monetary Damages**

Monetary damages can be sought to compensate for the financial losses incurred as a result of the breach of confidentiality. Types of damages that may be claimed include:

- **Actual Damages**: Compensation for the direct financial losses caused by the breach, such as lost profits, decreased market value, or costs incurred to mitigate the damage.
- **Unjust Enrichment**: Damages for any profits or benefits gained by the breaching party from the unauthorized use of confidential information.
- **Reasonable Royalty**: In some cases, the court may award damages based on a reasonable royalty for the unauthorized use of the confidential information.
- **Exemplary Damages**: In cases of willful and malicious misappropriation, courts may award exemplary damages of up to twice the amount of actual damages.

3. **Recover Legal Costs and Attorney's Fees**

   Under the Defend Trade Secrets Act (DTSA) and many state trade secret laws, the prevailing party may be entitled to recover legal costs and attorney's fees. This can provide significant financial relief and serves as a deterrent against frivolous lawsuits or malicious conduct.

4. **Seek Civil Seizure Orders**

   The DTSA provides a unique remedy in the form of civil seizure orders, which allow a court to seize property to prevent the dissemination of trade secrets in extraordinary circumstances:

   o **Application for Seizure**: The trade secret owner can apply for a civil seizure order, demonstrating that immediate and irreparable harm will occur if the property is not seized.
   o **Court-Ordered Seizure**: If granted, law enforcement will execute the seizure to recover the property containing the trade secrets, such as computer files, documents, or digital devices. The court then holds a hearing to determine the appropriate next steps.

5. **File Criminal Charges**

   In cases involving theft, fraud, or other criminal conduct, businesses may file criminal charges against the individuals or entities responsible for the breach. Under the Economic Espionage Act (EEA) and the DTSA, trade secret theft is a federal crime, and violators can face significant penalties, including:

   o **Fines**: Individuals convicted of trade secret theft can face fines up to $250,000, while organizations may face fines up to $5 million or more.
   o **Imprisonment**: Individuals convicted of trade secret theft may face up to 10 years in prison, depending on the severity of the offense.
   o **Restitution**: Courts may order defendants to pay restitution to the victim for the financial losses suffered due to the theft.

Chapter 5:

Avoiding Infringements and Defending Against Claims in the United States

This chapter focuses on strategies to help businesses and individuals avoid infringing on others' intellectual property (IP) rights and defend against potential infringement claims. A proactive approach to understanding the IP landscape is crucial to mitigating risks, reducing legal liabilities, and ensuring smooth business operations.

Conducting Preemptive Research on Existing IP Rights

Before launching a new product, service, or brand, it is essential to conduct thorough research on existing IP rights to ensure that you are not inadvertently infringing on another's patents, trademarks, or copyrights. This section explains the various methods for searching and analyzing existing IP rights and provides practical guidance on conducting effective searches.

Methods for Searching Existing Patents, Trademarks, and Copyrights

Conducting comprehensive searches for existing IP rights involves using specialized tools, databases, and professional services to identify registered or pending patents, trademarks, and copyrights that could potentially conflict with your IP. Here are the key methods for each type of IP:

1. Searching for Existing Patents

Patents grant inventors exclusive rights to their inventions and cover new processes, machines, compositions of matter, and designs. To avoid infringing on existing patents, consider the following steps:

- **Use the USPTO Patent Search Tools**:

  The United States Patent and Trademark Office (USPTO) provides several tools for searching existing patents:

- o **PatFT (Patent Full-Text and Image Database)**: This database allows users to search U.S. patents from 1790 to the present. You can search by keyword, patent number, classification, inventor name, assignee, or date.
- o **AppFT (Patent Application Full-Text and Image Database)**: This database enables searches of published patent applications from March 2001 onwards, providing insight into pending applications that could become patents.
- o **CPC Classification Search**: The Cooperative Patent Classification (CPC) system is used by the USPTO and the European Patent Office (EPO) to categorize patents by technical content. Searching by CPC codes can help locate patents within specific technological fields.

- **Use International Patent Databases**:

  For inventions that may require global protection or to check for potential infringements in other jurisdictions, use international patent databases such as:

  - o **WIPO PATENTSCOPE**: Provided by the World Intellectual Property Organization (WIPO), this database includes published international patent applications filed under the Patent Cooperation Treaty (PCT) and national collections from participating patent offices.
  - o **Espacenet**: Managed by the EPO, this database offers access to over 120 million patent documents worldwide. Espacenet allows users to search by keywords, applicant names, classifications, and other criteria.

- **Conduct Prior Art Searches**:

  A prior art search involves identifying any existing patents, publications, or disclosures that may be relevant to your invention:

  - o **Keyword Searches**: Use keywords related to your invention's technical features, functions, or applications to locate similar patents or applications.

- o **Patent Citation Analysis**: Review patent citations in relevant patents to identify related prior art and understand the patent landscape in your field.

- **Hire Professional Patent Search Services**:

  Consider hiring professional patent search firms or patent attorneys to conduct thorough prior art searches, particularly for complex inventions. These professionals have expertise in patent law, technical knowledge, and access to specialized search tools.

2. Searching for Existing Trademarks

Trademarks protect brand names, logos, slogans, and other identifiers that distinguish goods or services. To avoid infringing on existing trademarks, follow these steps:

- **Use the USPTO Trademark Electronic Search System (TESS)**:

  The USPTO's TESS database allows users to search for registered and pending trademarks:

  - o **Basic Word Mark Search**: Conduct a basic search by entering keywords related to the trademark you intend to use. This can help identify exact matches or similar marks.
  - o **Advanced Search Options**: Use the advanced search features to filter results by owner, registration date, filing date, or International Class. You can also search by design elements using the Design Search Code Manual.
  - o **Trademark Status and Document Retrieval (TSDR)**: Use TSDR to check the status, registration history, and related documents of specific trademarks.

- **Search International Trademark Databases**:

  For global business or international expansion, use international trademark databases to check for potential conflicts:

  - o **WIPO Global Brand Database**: This database includes registered trademarks, appellations of origin, and official emblems from multiple jurisdictions. It provides an easy way to check for trademarks across different countries.

- o **Madrid Monitor**: Provided by WIPO, Madrid Monitor allows users to search trademarks registered under the Madrid System, a centralized trademark registration system for international protection.

- **Search Common Law Trademarks**:

In the United States, trademark rights can be established through use in commerce without registration. To search for common law trademarks:

- o **Use Commercial Search Services**: Services like Corsearch or Thomson CompuMark provide access to comprehensive trademark databases, including common law marks.
- o **Conduct Internet Searches**: Perform searches on major search engines, business directories, and social media platforms to identify unregistered trademarks in use.

- **Hire a Trademark Attorney**:

A trademark attorney can conduct more thorough searches, provide legal opinions on potential conflicts, and advise on strategies to minimize infringement risks.

3. Searching for Existing Copyrights

Copyrights protect original works of authorship, such as literature, music, art, films, software, and more. To avoid copyright infringement, consider the following steps:

- **Use the U.S. Copyright Office Public Catalog**:

The U.S. Copyright Office provides an online Public Catalog that allows users to search for registered copyrights:

- o **Basic Search**: Enter keywords, author names, titles, or registration numbers to find registered works.
- o **Advanced Search**: Use advanced search options to filter results by type of work (e.g., literary, visual, performing arts), registration date, or copyright owner.

- **Search Creative Commons and Public Domain Repositories**:

  To avoid using copyrighted works without permission, consider using works available under Creative Commons licenses or those in the public domain:

  - **Creative Commons Search**: A search tool that indexes works licensed under Creative Commons, making them freely available for specific uses.
  - **Public Domain Resources**: Use platforms like Project Gutenberg, Wikimedia Commons, or the Internet Archive to find public domain works that are free from copyright restrictions.

- **Check Stock Photo and Music Libraries**:

  For images, music, and other creative assets, use licensed stock libraries like Getty Images, Shutterstock, or AudioJungle to ensure you are using content legally.

- **Hire Copyright Research Services**:

  For complex projects involving multiple copyrighted works, consider hiring professional services that specialize in copyright clearance and licensing.

Best Practices for Conducting Comprehensive IP Searches

1. **Use Multiple Search Tools and Databases**

   Use a combination of national and international databases, public and commercial search tools, and professional services to ensure a comprehensive search. Different tools provide different coverage and capabilities, and using multiple sources increases the likelihood of identifying potential conflicts.

2. **Refine Your Search Criteria**

   Start with broad search terms and gradually narrow them down to focus on specific areas of interest. Use synonyms, related terms, and variations to cover all possible matches.

3. **Document Your Search Process**

   Keep detailed records of your search process, including the databases used, search terms, and results. This documentation can serve as evidence of due diligence in the event of an infringement claim.

4. **Consult with IP Professionals**

   Work with IP attorneys or specialists to interpret search results, assess the risk of potential conflicts, and develop strategies to minimize infringement risks. Professionals can provide legal opinions and advice tailored to your specific situation.

Defensive Strategies Against Infringement Claims (5-6 pages)

When faced with an infringement claim, it is crucial to know the legal defenses available under U.S. law. These defenses can help mitigate or entirely nullify claims of infringement, depending on the specific circumstances of the case. The most common defenses include "fair use" and "fair dealing," among others. Additionally, understanding relevant case studies and legal strategies can provide insights into how these defenses are applied in practice.

Common Defenses Like "Fair Use" and "Fair Dealing" in the U.S.

1. Fair Use Defense

The "fair use" doctrine is one of the most significant defenses against copyright infringement claims in the United States. It allows limited use of copyrighted material without the owner's permission, provided the use meets certain criteria.

- **Definition of Fair Use**:

  Fair use permits the unlicensed use of copyrighted material for specific purposes such as criticism, comment, news reporting, teaching, scholarship, or research. The doctrine is codified in Section 107 of the U.S. Copyright Act, which outlines four factors that courts consider when determining whether a use qualifies as fair use:

- **Purpose and Character of the Use**: This factor examines whether the use is of a commercial nature or for nonprofit educational purposes. Courts are more likely to find fair use when the purpose is transformative—meaning it adds new expression, meaning, or message to the original work. For example, using a copyrighted image in a parody that comments on the original work is more likely to be considered fair use than using it in an advertisement.
- **Nature of the Copyrighted Work**: This factor considers whether the work is factual or creative. Courts generally afford less protection to factual works (like news articles) than to creative works (like novels or movies). Additionally, unpublished works are less likely to be considered fair use since the owner has not yet exercised the right to control its first public appearance.
- **Amount and Substantiality of the Portion Used**: This factor evaluates both the quantity and the qualitative significance of the portion used in relation to the copyrighted work as a whole. Using small excerpts of a work may favor fair use, especially if the use does not capture the "heart" of the work.
- **Effect of the Use on the Market for the Original Work**: This factor assesses whether the unlicensed use negatively impacts the market for or value of the original work. If the use harms the potential market or serves as a substitute for the original work, it is less likely to be considered fair use.

- **Applications of Fair Use**:

  Fair use is a flexible standard applied on a case-by-case basis. Some common examples of uses that may qualify as fair use include:

  - **Commentary and Criticism**: Using excerpts from a book, movie, or other work in a critical review or commentary.
  - **Parody**: Imitating or mimicking a work in a way that comments on or ridicules the original.

103

- o **Educational Use**: Reproducing small portions of a work for classroom teaching, academic research, or scholarship.
- o **News Reporting**: Quoting or showing portions of copyrighted works in news broadcasts or articles.

2. Fair Dealing Defense

While "fair dealing" is not a specific defense under U.S. law, it is a related concept used in other common law jurisdictions, such as the United Kingdom and Canada. However, in the U.S., the idea of fair dealing is generally subsumed under fair use.

- • **Key Differences Between Fair Use and Fair Dealing**:

  Fair use in the U.S. is broader and more flexible than fair dealing in other jurisdictions. Fair dealing typically applies only to specific, enumerated purposes (e.g., research, private study, criticism, or review). In contrast, fair use can be applied to a wider range of purposes and is evaluated based on the four factors mentioned above.

3. Other Common Defenses Against Infringement Claims

- • **Invalidity or Unenforceability**: This defense argues that the IP in question is invalid or unenforceable due to defects in registration or a failure to meet statutory requirements. For example, a patent could be invalidated if it was improperly granted due to a lack of novelty or non-obviousness.
- • **Statutory Exemptions**: Some IP laws provide specific exemptions that allow certain uses without constituting infringement. For example, Section 512 of the Digital Millennium Copyright Act (DMCA) provides a "safe harbor" for internet service providers (ISPs) from liability for user-generated content, provided they comply with notice and takedown procedures.
- • **Non-Infringing Use**: This defense asserts that the accused activity does not actually constitute infringement. For instance, in patent law, the defense might argue that the allegedly infringing product does not fall within the scope of the patent's claims.

- **First Sale Doctrine**: This doctrine allows the lawful purchaser of a copyrighted work to resell or distribute that specific copy without the copyright holder's permission, provided the initial sale was authorized. For example, a person who buys a book is free to resell it without infringing the author's copyright.
- **License or Consent**: The defendant may argue that they had a license (express or implied) or consent from the IP holder to use the protected work. This defense focuses on the existence of an agreement permitting the use.

Case Studies and Legal Strategies

Understanding how these defenses have been applied in real-world cases can provide valuable insights into effective legal strategies. Here are some notable case studies:

Case Study 1: Fair Use in Transformative Works

- **Case**: *Campbell v. Acuff-Rose Music, Inc. (1994)*
- **Background**: In this landmark case, the rap group 2 Live Crew created a parody of Roy Orbison's song "Oh, Pretty Woman." Acuff-Rose Music, the copyright holder, sued for infringement.
- **Defense Strategy**: 2 Live Crew argued that their song was a parody and thus a transformative use that qualified as fair use.
- **Outcome**: The U.S. Supreme Court ruled in favor of 2 Live Crew, stating that parody can be considered fair use if it adds new expression or meaning to the original work and does not serve as a substitute. The Court emphasized the importance of the "transformative" nature of the work in assessing fair use.

Case Study 2: Fair Use in News Reporting

- **Case**: *Associated Press v. Meltwater U.S. Holdings, Inc. (2013)*
- **Background**: Meltwater, a news aggregation service, was sued by the Associated Press (AP) for reproducing portions of AP's articles without permission.
- **Defense Strategy**: Meltwater claimed that its use was fair use, as it was providing summaries and snippets for public information purposes.

- **Outcome**: The court ruled against Meltwater, finding that its use was not transformative and that it directly competed with AP's licensed products. The decision underscored the importance of assessing the purpose and market impact of the use.

Case Study 3: Invalidity Defense in Patent Litigation

- **Case**: *Microsoft Corp. v. i4i Limited Partnership (2011)*
- **Background**: Microsoft was sued for infringing a patent owned by i4i related to XML technology. Microsoft argued that the patent was invalid due to prior art that i4i had failed to disclose to the USPTO.
- **Defense Strategy**: Microsoft employed the invalidity defense, contending that the patent should not have been granted in the first place.
- **Outcome**: The U.S. Supreme Court upheld the lower court's ruling in favor of i4i, affirming that a patent must be proven invalid by "clear and convincing evidence." The case highlighted the high burden of proof required for the invalidity defense.

Legal Strategies for Defending Against Infringement Claims

1. **Conduct a Thorough Prior Art Search**

   For patent cases, a comprehensive prior art search can uncover existing patents, publications, or public uses that may render the patent invalid. This strategy can help build a strong invalidity defense.

2. **Demonstrate Transformative Use**

   In copyright cases, focus on demonstrating that the use is transformative—adding new meaning, message, or purpose to the original work. Highlight any social, educational, or critical aspects that support fair use.

3. **Challenge the Scope of Protection**

   Analyze the scope of the IP claims being asserted and argue that the alleged infringing activity does not fall within this scope. This is particularly relevant in patent cases, where the interpretation of claims can be contested.

4. **Gather Evidence of Licenses or Permissions**

    Collect all relevant documentation showing that the defendant had a license or permission to use the IP. This can include written agreements, emails, or any communications indicating consent.

5. **Negotiate Settlements or Licensing Agreements**

    In some cases, negotiating a settlement or licensing agreement may be a more cost-effective and practical solution than prolonged litigation. This strategy can help avoid the uncertainty and expenses of a court trial.

By understanding these common defenses and employing effective legal strategies, businesses and individuals can better protect themselves against IP infringement claims and navigate complex legal challenges with confidence.

Resolving Intellectual Property Disputes

Resolving IP disputes through negotiation and other out-of-court methods is often preferable to litigation, which can be costly, time-consuming, and adversarial. This section covers best practices for negotiating agreements, using ADR mechanisms like mediation and arbitration, and employing conflict resolution strategies to settle disputes amicably.

Negotiating Agreements and Conflict Resolution Without Litigation

1. Understanding the Benefits of Non-Litigation Approaches

Using negotiation and ADR methods to resolve IP disputes offers several advantages over litigation:

- **Cost-Effective**: Negotiation and ADR can significantly reduce legal expenses and other costs associated with court proceedings. Litigation often involves attorney fees, court fees, expert witness fees, and extensive discovery processes, which can be financially draining.

- **Time-Saving**: Resolving disputes outside of court can be much faster than litigation, which can take months or even years. ADR methods like mediation or arbitration can often be scheduled and completed within weeks or months.
- **Confidentiality**: Unlike court cases, which are typically public, ADR proceedings and negotiations are usually private. This confidentiality can protect sensitive business information, trade secrets, and reputations.
- **Preservation of Business Relationships**: Negotiation and ADR provide a more collaborative approach to dispute resolution, which can help preserve and even strengthen business relationships. Parties are more likely to reach mutually beneficial solutions and continue working together.
- **Flexibility in Solutions**: Courts are limited in the remedies they can provide, usually focusing on damages or injunctions. Negotiation and ADR offer more flexibility, allowing parties to craft creative, customized solutions that meet their specific needs.

2. Negotiation Techniques for IP Disputes

Negotiation is often the first step in attempting to resolve an IP dispute. Effective negotiation strategies can help both parties reach an agreement that avoids litigation:

- **Preparation and Research**: Thoroughly prepare for negotiations by gathering all relevant information, including the IP at issue, the parties' respective rights, and any prior communications or agreements. Understand your own objectives, as well as those of the other party, and anticipate potential points of contention.
- **Define Clear Objectives and Bottom Lines**: Know what you want to achieve from the negotiation and what you are willing to concede. Establish clear objectives and identify your bottom line—the minimum acceptable outcome you are willing to accept. This helps guide your negotiation strategy and prevents you from making unfavorable concessions.

- **Build Rapport and Foster Open Communication**: Establish a cooperative environment by building rapport and trust with the other party. Encourage open communication by actively listening, acknowledging the other party's concerns, and expressing your interests clearly and respectfully.
- **Focus on Interests, Not Positions**: Negotiating based on interests rather than rigid positions allows for more creative problem-solving. Understand the underlying needs, motivations, and interests of both parties to find common ground and develop mutually beneficial solutions.
- **Use Objective Criteria**: Rely on objective standards, such as industry norms, market rates, or legal precedents, to support your positions and demands. This helps ensure that negotiations are fair and reasonable and prevents disputes from becoming overly subjective or emotional.
- **Propose Win-Win Solutions**: Aim for outcomes that benefit both parties. Consider offering concessions that are less important to you but highly valuable to the other party, and vice versa. Explore creative solutions that address the interests of both sides, such as cross-licensing, joint ventures, or royalty agreements.
- **Prepare for Impasses and Deadlocks**: Be prepared to handle impasses or deadlocks in negotiations. Consider using techniques like breaking down the negotiation into smaller, more manageable parts, proposing alternative options, or agreeing to "pause and reconvene" to give both parties time to reassess their positions.
- **Draft a Settlement Agreement**: Once an agreement is reached, document the terms in a written settlement agreement that outlines the rights, obligations, and responsibilities of each party. Ensure the agreement is clear, comprehensive, and legally binding to avoid future misunderstandings or disputes.

3. Alternative Dispute Resolution (ADR) Methods for IP Disputes

If direct negotiation fails to resolve the dispute, parties may turn to Alternative Dispute Resolution (ADR) methods, such as mediation and arbitration, to settle their differences without going to court.

- **Mediation**:

  Mediation is a voluntary and confidential process where a neutral third party, the mediator, facilitates communication between the disputing parties to help them reach a mutually acceptable agreement. Mediation is non-binding, meaning the mediator does not have the authority to impose a decision; instead, the mediator helps the parties explore solutions.

  - **Advantages of Mediation:**
    1. **Preserves Relationships**: Mediation fosters open communication and collaboration, which can help maintain business relationships.
    2. **Control over Outcome**: Parties retain control over the outcome and can agree to terms that best suit their needs.
    3. **Cost-Effective and Efficient**: Mediation is generally less expensive and faster than litigation.
  - **Mediation Process:**
    4. **Selection of Mediator**: Choose a qualified mediator experienced in IP disputes.
    5. **Pre-Mediation Preparation**: Each party prepares a brief outlining their position, interests, and desired outcomes.
    6. **Mediation Sessions**: The mediator facilitates discussions, encourages dialogue, and helps parties identify potential areas of agreement.
    7. **Reaching an Agreement**: If an agreement is reached, the mediator helps draft a written settlement. If no agreement is reached, parties may pursue other remedies.

- **Arbitration**:

  Arbitration is a formal ADR process where the disputing parties agree to submit their dispute to one or more arbitrators who render a binding decision. Unlike mediation, arbitration results in a legally enforceable award that both parties must adhere to.

- o **Advantages of Arbitration:**
  1. **Binding Decision**: The decision (award) is binding and enforceable in court.
  2. **Neutral Expertise**: Arbitrators with specific expertise in IP law can be selected.
  3. **Confidentiality**: Arbitration proceedings are private, and the details of the dispute and award are usually confidential.
  4. **Flexibility**: Parties can agree on procedural rules, venue, and timelines.
- o **Arbitration Process:**
  5. **Agreement to Arbitrate**: Parties must agree to arbitrate, either through a pre-existing arbitration clause in a contract or by mutual consent after a dispute arises.
  6. **Selection of Arbitrator(s)**: Parties select one or more arbitrators, typically with expertise in IP law.
  7. **Arbitration Hearing**: Both parties present evidence, witnesses, and arguments to the arbitrator(s).
  8. **Arbitrator's Decision**: The arbitrator(s) render a binding decision (award), which can be enforced in court if necessary.

4. Conflict Resolution Strategies in IP Disputes

In addition to negotiation and ADR, there are several strategies to help resolve IP disputes effectively:

- **Engage in Early Case Assessment (ECA)**: Before escalating a dispute, conduct an early case assessment to evaluate the strengths and weaknesses of your position, the potential risks, and the costs of litigation versus settlement. This assessment can guide decision-making on whether to negotiate, mediate, or arbitrate.
- **Utilize a Neutral Evaluation**: Consider a neutral evaluation, where an independent expert evaluates the merits of the dispute and provides a non-binding assessment. This can help both

parties understand the likely outcome if the case goes to court and may encourage settlement.

- **Propose a Standstill Agreement**: In cases where parties wish to pause legal proceedings and explore settlement options, propose a standstill agreement. This agreement temporarily halts any ongoing litigation or arbitration while negotiations take place.
- **Consider Joint IP Committees**: In long-term business relationships, consider forming joint IP committees to proactively manage potential disputes. These committees can establish guidelines for IP use, resolve disagreements early, and prevent disputes from escalating.
- **Leverage Technology in Dispute Resolution**: Use technology, such as online dispute resolution (ODR) platforms, to facilitate communication, share documents, and manage the negotiation or ADR process more efficiently.

Sample Legal Documents and Agreements

Legal documents play a vital role in managing IP disputes and protecting IP rights. This section includes examples of key documents such as warning letters, licensing agreements, and settlement documents. Understanding the purpose and structure of these documents can help parties navigate IP conflicts more effectively.

Examples of Warning Letters, Licensing Agreements, and Settlement Documents

1. Warning Letter (Cease and Desist Letter)

A warning letter, also known as a cease and desist letter, is often the first step taken to address a suspected IP infringement. It is sent by the IP owner to the alleged infringer, demanding that they stop the infringing activity and take corrective actions.

Purpose: The goal of a warning letter is to notify the alleged infringer of their unauthorized use of the IP, assert the owner's rights, and demand cessation of the infringing activities without resorting to litigation.

Key Elements of a Warning Letter:

- **Header**: Include the sender's and recipient's names, addresses, and the date of the letter.
- **Introduction**: Briefly introduce the sender (IP owner) and outline the purpose of the letter.
- **Description of the Infringement**: Provide a detailed description of the alleged infringement, including the specific IP rights (e.g., trademark, patent, copyright) that have been violated.
- **Assertion of Rights**: Clearly state the sender's rights to the IP and their intent to enforce those rights.
- **Demand for Cessation**: Specify the actions the recipient must take to cease the infringing activities, such as stopping the use, sale, or distribution of the infringing products.
- **Deadline for Compliance**: Set a reasonable deadline (e.g., 14 days) for the recipient to comply with the demands or respond to the letter.
- **Consequences of Non-Compliance**: Outline the potential legal consequences of failing to comply with the demands, including litigation, damages, and attorney's fees.
- **Contact Information**: Provide contact details for further communication or resolution.
- **Closing**: Conclude with a formal closing and the sender's signature.

Sample Warning Letter:

[Sender's Letterhead]
[Sender's Name]
[Sender's Address]
[City, State, ZIP Code]
[Date]

[Recipient's Name]
[Recipient's Address]
[City, State, ZIP Code]

Subject: Cease and Desist Notice – Unauthorized Use of [Trademark/Patent/Copyright]

Dear [Recipient's Name],

We are writing on behalf of [Your Company], the rightful owner of [describe the IP, e.g., the trademark "BrandName" registered under U.S. Reg. No. 1234567]. It has come to our attention that your company, [Recipient's Company], is [describe the infringing activity, e.g., using a similar mark "Brand X" in a manner that is likely to cause confusion among consumers].

This unauthorized use constitutes a violation of our exclusive rights under the [U.S. Trademark Act/U.S. Copyright Act/Patent Act]. We demand that you immediately cease all infringing activities, including [list specific actions, e.g., removing the infringing mark from all products, websites, and marketing materials].

Please confirm in writing by [date, e.g., 14 days from the date of this letter] that you have complied with our demands. If we do not receive a satisfactory response by this date, we will be compelled to pursue all legal remedies available to us, including filing a lawsuit seeking injunctive relief, damages, and recovery of attorney's fees.

We hope to resolve this matter amicably without resorting to litigation. Should you wish to discuss this matter further, please contact me at [email or phone number].

Sincerely,
[Your Name]
[Your Title]
[Your Company]

Licensing Agreement

A licensing agreement is a contract between an IP owner (licensor) and another party (licensee) that grants the licensee the right to use the IP under specific terms and conditions. This agreement is often used to settle disputes by allowing the alleged infringer to continue using the IP legally in exchange for compensation.

Purpose: To formalize the terms under which the licensee may use the licensor's IP, specify the scope of usage, and outline payment terms, royalties, and other obligations.

Key Elements of a Licensing Agreement:

- **Parties**: Identify the licensor and licensee, including their legal names and addresses.
- **Grant of License**: Clearly define the rights being licensed (e.g., exclusive or non-exclusive, territory, duration) and the scope of use (e.g., specific products or services).
- **Payment Terms**: Specify the compensation structure, including upfront fees, royalties, minimum payments, and payment schedule.
- **Obligations of the Licensee**: Outline the licensee's obligations, such as quality control, compliance with laws, and restrictions on sublicensing or assignment.
- **IP Ownership and Protection**: Affirm that the licensor retains all ownership rights to the IP and describe the licensee's responsibilities in protecting those rights.
- **Termination**: Specify the conditions under which the agreement can be terminated, including breach of contract, non-payment, or expiration of the term.
- **Dispute Resolution**: Include provisions for resolving disputes, such as negotiation, mediation, or arbitration.
- **Confidentiality**: Address the confidentiality of the agreement and any related information.
- **Signatures**: Provide spaces for the signatures of authorized representatives from both parties.
-

Sample Licensing Agreement:

LICENSE AGREEMENT

This License Agreement ("Agreement") is entered into on [Date], by and between:

Licensor: [Licensor's Name], having its principal place of business at [Licensor's Address].

Licensee: [Licensee's Name], having its principal place of business at [Licensee's Address].

1. Grant of License
   Licensor hereby grants to Licensee a [non-exclusive/exclusive] license to use the [trademark/patent/copyright] identified as [describe IP, e.g., "BrandName"] in connection with [describe use, e.g., the sale of specific products] within the territory of [define territory].

2. Term and Termination
   This Agreement shall commence on [start date] and continue for a period of [define duration], unless terminated earlier in accordance with the terms herein.

3. Payment Terms
   Licensee agrees to pay Licensor an upfront fee of [$ amount] and royalties of [percentage]% of net sales, payable [quarterly/annually] within [number of days] days of each reporting period.

4. Obligations of Licensee
   Licensee shall [outline specific obligations, e.g., maintain quality standards, provide sales reports, etc.].

5. Intellectual Property Ownership
   Licensor retains all ownership rights to the [trademark/patent/copyright], and Licensee shall take no action inconsistent with Licensor's rights.

6. Confidentiality
   Both parties agree to maintain the confidentiality of all proprietary and confidential information disclosed under this Agreement.

7. Governing Law and Dispute Resolution
   This Agreement shall be governed by the laws of [State/Country]. Any disputes arising under this Agreement shall be resolved through [negotiation/mediation/arbitration].

IN WITNESS WHEREOF, the parties have executed this License Agreement as of the Effective Date.

[Licensor's Signature]
[Licensor's Name, Title]

[Licensee's Signature]
[Licensee's Name, Title]

Settlement Agreement

A settlement agreement is a legally binding document that outlines the terms under which the parties agree to resolve a dispute, often to avoid litigation. This agreement formalizes the resolution of an IP dispute, including any payments, licenses, or changes in conduct required to settle the matter.

Purpose: To clearly define the terms of settlement, ensure compliance, and prevent future disputes over the same issue.

Key Elements of a Settlement Agreement:

- **Parties**: Identify the parties involved in the dispute and their legal representatives.
- **Recitals**: Provide background information on the dispute, the claims made, and the reasons for reaching a settlement.
- **Terms of Settlement**: Detail the specific terms, such as payment amounts, licensing terms, cessation of activities, and any other obligations.
- **Release of Claims**: Include a release clause stating that the parties waive any future claims related to the dispute.
- **Confidentiality**: Include a confidentiality clause to keep the terms of the settlement private.
- **Non-Disparagement**: Prohibit the parties from making any negative statements about each other.
- **Dispute Resolution and Governing Law**: Outline procedures for resolving any future disputes related to the settlement.
- **Signatures**: Provide spaces for the signatures of all parties and their representatives.

Sample Settlement Agreement:

SETTLEMENT AGREEMENT

This Settlement Agreement ("Agreement") is entered into as of [Date] by and between:

Party A: [Party A's Name], having its principal place of business at [Party A's Address].

Party B: [Party B's Name], having its principal place of business at [Party B's Address].

WHEREAS, Party A and Party B have been engaged in a dispute concerning [describe dispute, e.g., alleged infringement of a patent], and desire to resolve this matter without further litigation.

NOW, THEREFORE, the parties agree as follows:

1. Settlement Terms
   Party A agrees to [specific terms, e.g., make a one-time payment of $X to Party B]. Party B agrees to [specific terms, e.g., cease all production and sale of the disputed product].

2. Release of Claims
   Each party releases the other from any and all claims related to the dispute as of the date of this Agreement.

3. Confidentiality
   The parties agree that the terms of this Agreement shall remain confidential and shall not be disclosed to any third parties except as required by law.

4. Non-Disparagement
   The parties agree not to make any public or private statements that disparage the other party or its business practices.

5. Dispute Resolution
   Any disputes arising from this Agreement shall be resolved through [negotiation/mediation/arbitration] in accordance with the laws of [State/Country].

IN WITNESS WHEREOF, the parties hereto have executed this Settlement Agreement as of the date first above written.

[Party A's Signature]
[Party A's Name, Title]

[Party B's Signature]
[Party B's Name, Title]

Chapter 6:

Utilizing Intellectual Property on the Internet in the United States

This chapter provides guidance on how to protect and manage intellectual property (IP) in the digital age, focusing on strategies for safeguarding copyright and other types of IP when they are used or shared online. As businesses increasingly rely on the internet for content distribution, marketing, and sales, understanding how to protect digital assets is more important than ever.

Protecting Digital Copyright and Online Content (5-6 pages)

Copyright protection is crucial in the digital environment, where content can be easily copied, distributed, and shared across various platforms. This section offers best practices for safeguarding copyrighted works, such as literary texts, images, videos, software, and other online content. These strategies can help creators, businesses, and IP owners protect their rights and minimize the risk of unauthorized use or infringement.

Best Practices for Safeguarding Copyright Online

1. Register Copyrights with the U.S. Copyright Office

While copyright protection is automatically granted upon creation of a work, registering the copyright with the U.S. Copyright Office provides additional legal benefits, including:

- **Public Record**: Registration establishes a public record of ownership, which is crucial for asserting rights and claiming infringement.
- **Legal Presumption of Ownership**: Registration provides prima facie evidence of the validity of the copyright and ownership, making it easier to enforce rights in court.
- **Eligibility for Statutory Damages and Attorney's Fees**: If a copyright is registered before an infringement occurs or within

three months of publication, the owner may be eligible for statutory damages and attorney's fees, which can significantly enhance the ability to seek compensation.

Action Steps:

- Register all digital content, including text, images, videos, music, and software, with the U.S. Copyright Office.
- Keep accurate records of the registration, including certificates and application details.

2. Use Digital Watermarking and Metadata

Digital watermarking and metadata embedding are effective tools for protecting copyrighted content online:

- **Digital Watermarking**: A digital watermark is a visible or invisible mark embedded into a digital file (such as an image, video, or document) that identifies the owner or source. Watermarks can deter unauthorized use by clearly indicating ownership.

  - **Visible Watermarks**: Logos, text, or graphics added to images or videos that indicate copyright ownership. For example, placing a company logo in the corner of a photo.
  - **Invisible Watermarks**: Data embedded within the file that is not visible to users but can be detected by specialized software to prove ownership or trace unauthorized use.

- **Metadata**: Metadata is information embedded in digital files that describes the content, author, copyright status, and usage terms.

  - **IPTC Metadata**: Use the International Press Telecommunications Council (IPTC) metadata standards to embed copyright information in images, such as the creator's name, contact details, and copyright notice.
  - **EXIF Data**: For photographs, use Exchangeable Image File Format (EXIF) data to store copyright information, capture date, camera settings, and other details.

Action Steps:

- Embed digital watermarks in all online content, especially images and videos.
- Use metadata to provide clear copyright information and usage terms for all digital files.
- Regularly check that metadata remains intact and has not been removed or altered by unauthorized users.

3. Implement Technical Protection Measures (TPMs)

Technical Protection Measures (TPMs) are technologies that control access to or use of copyrighted works:

- **Digital Rights Management (DRM)**: DRM technologies restrict how digital content can be used, copied, or distributed. They are commonly used for e-books, music, software, and videos to prevent unauthorized access or duplication.

  o **Access Control**: DRM can restrict access to content based on user credentials, device restrictions, or geographical locations.

  o **Usage Control**: DRM can limit the number of times content can be accessed, downloaded, or printed.

- **Password Protection and Encryption**: Use password protection and encryption for documents, software, or multimedia content to prevent unauthorized access.

  o **Encryption**: Encrypt sensitive files and communications to protect against interception or unauthorized decryption.

Action Steps:

- Use DRM services to manage and enforce access controls for online content, such as e-books, videos, and music.
- Implement strong password protection and encryption methods for content shared or stored online.
- Regularly update and review TPMs to ensure they remain effective against new threats.

4. Monitor the Internet for Infringements

Proactive monitoring of the internet is essential to identify and address unauthorized use of copyrighted content:

- **Set Up Google Alerts**: Use Google Alerts to monitor the internet for specific keywords related to your copyrighted works. Alerts will notify you whenever the content appears online.
- **Use Reverse Image Search**: Use tools like Google Reverse Image Search or TinEye to find unauthorized copies of your images or photographs across the web.
- **Employ Digital Fingerprinting**: Digital fingerprinting involves creating a unique identifier or "fingerprint" for each piece of content. Services such as YouTube's Content ID use fingerprinting to detect unauthorized copies of videos or audio.
- **Monitor Social Media**: Regularly check social media platforms for unauthorized sharing or distribution of copyrighted content.

Action Steps:

- Set up alerts and use reverse search tools to proactively monitor for potential infringements.
- Consider using specialized monitoring services, such as DMCA.com, Copytrack, or Pixsy, that offer automated detection and takedown services.

5. Utilize the Digital Millennium Copyright Act (DMCA)

The DMCA provides a framework for content owners to request the removal of infringing content from websites, search engines, and online platforms:

- **Send DMCA Takedown Notices**: When you discover infringing content, you can send a DMCA takedown notice to the website hosting the content or the service provider (e.g., Google, YouTube). The notice should include:

  o A description of the copyrighted work.
  o The location (URL) of the infringing material.
  o A statement of good faith belief that the use is unauthorized.
  o Your contact information and a signature.

- **Follow Up on Takedown Notices**: After sending a DMCA notice, monitor the situation to ensure that the infringing content is removed. If necessary, follow up with the service provider or seek legal counsel if they do not comply.

Action Steps:

- Familiarize yourself with the DMCA's requirements and process for sending takedown notices.
- Use standardized DMCA templates to streamline the takedown process.
- Maintain records of all notices sent and any responses received.

6. Leverage Licensing Agreements and Online Marketplaces

Use licensing agreements and online platforms to control how your content is distributed and monetized:

- **Licensing Agreements**: Grant licenses to authorized users or platforms to use your content under specific terms and conditions, such as payment of royalties, attribution, or use restrictions.
- **Utilize Content Platforms**: Distribute content through platforms that offer built-in protections, such as iTunes, Amazon Kindle Direct Publishing (KDP), Shutterstock, or Adobe Stock. These platforms have their own enforcement mechanisms to prevent unauthorized distribution.

Action Steps:

- Draft clear and comprehensive licensing agreements for all third-party use of your content.
- Select reputable platforms with strong IP protection policies for distributing your digital content.

7. Educate Your Team and Partners

Ensure that everyone involved in creating, managing, and distributing your online content understands copyright laws and best practices:

- **Employee Training**: Train employees and collaborators on copyright basics, internal IP policies, and how to handle unauthorized use of content.
- **Partner Agreements**: Include IP protection clauses in contracts with partners, vendors, and freelancers, specifying their responsibilities in safeguarding your content.

Action Steps:

- Conduct regular training sessions on copyright protection and digital rights management.
- Review and update contracts and agreements with third parties to include IP protection clauses.

By implementing these best practices, creators, businesses, and IP owners can protect their digital content, assert their rights, and mitigate the risks of online infringement. This proactive approach ensures that valuable IP assets remain secure and that content creators receive fair compensation

Managing Domain Names and Protecting Trademarks Online (5-6 pages)

Domain names serve as the online identity for businesses, individuals, and organizations. They are often closely associated with a brand's trademark, making it essential to manage domain names strategically and protect them from unauthorized use. Effective management of domain names, combined with a robust trademark protection strategy, helps prevent brand dilution, consumer confusion, and loss of goodwill.

Understanding Domain Names and Trademarks

- **Domain Names**: A domain name is the address of a website on the internet, such as "example.com." It provides a unique identifier that allows users to access the website. Domain names often contain a brand name or trademark, making them a valuable asset for businesses.
- **Trademarks**: A trademark is a word, phrase, symbol, design, or combination thereof that identifies and distinguishes the source of goods or services. When used in domain names, trademarks

help build brand recognition and consumer trust. However, domain names and trademarks are governed by different legal frameworks, which can create complexities in protecting brand identity online.

Best Practices for Managing Domain Names

1. Choose Domain Names That Reflect Your Brand or Trademark

Select domain names that are closely aligned with your trademark or brand name. This strategy helps ensure consistency across your digital and offline presence and makes it easier for customers to find your website:

- **Use Clear and Recognizable Terms**: Choose domain names that use your exact trademark, brand name, or a common abbreviation. Avoid ambiguous or generic terms that could dilute your brand's identity.
- **Consider Multiple Variants**: Register common variations of your domain name, including different spellings, abbreviations, and top-level domains (TLDs) like ".com," ".net," ".org," ".co," and country-specific TLDs (e.g., ".us" or ".uk"). This prevents competitors or bad actors from using similar names to confuse consumers.
- **Monitor New TLDs**: Be aware of new generic TLDs (gTLDs) that could be relevant to your brand (e.g., ".shop," ".online," ".store"). Consider registering these domains to expand your online presence and protect against misuse.

2. Register and Renew Domain Names Promptly

Domain names must be registered with an accredited registrar and renewed regularly to maintain ownership:

- **Register Domain Names Early**: Register domain names as soon as possible to secure them and prevent competitors or cybersquatters from acquiring them.
- **Renew on Time**: Set up automatic renewals or reminders to ensure domain names do not expire. If a domain name lapses, it

could be acquired by another party, leading to loss of brand control and potential infringement.

- **Use a Trusted Registrar**: Choose a reputable domain registrar with a proven track record of security, reliability, and customer support. Consider registrars accredited by the Internet Corporation for Assigned Names and Numbers (ICANN).

3. Monitor Domain Name Use

Regular monitoring is crucial for detecting unauthorized use of domain names that may infringe on your trademark:

- **Set Up Alerts**: Use tools like Google Alerts or domain monitoring services to track mentions of your domain name, trademark, or similar terms online. This helps identify potential infringement or misuse by third parties.
- **Use Domain Name Monitoring Services**: Many registrars and specialized companies offer domain name monitoring services that notify you when new domains are registered containing your trademark or similar terms. These services can provide early warnings of potential cybersquatting or infringement.

4. Respond Promptly to Infringement or Cybersquatting

Cybersquatting, or the practice of registering domain names containing trademarks with the intent to profit, can damage a brand's reputation and cause consumer confusion. If you discover a domain name that infringes on your trademark:

- **Send a Cease and Desist Letter**: Contact the domain name owner with a cease and desist letter, demanding they stop using the infringing domain and transfer it to you. Be clear about your rights and provide evidence of your trademark ownership.
- **File a Complaint Under the UDRP or URS**: If the infringing party does not comply, consider filing a complaint under the Uniform Domain-Name Dispute-Resolution Policy (UDRP) or the Uniform Rapid Suspension System (URS). These mechanisms, administered by ICANN, provide a streamlined process for resolving disputes involving domain names.

o **UDRP**: The UDRP allows trademark owners to seek the transfer or cancellation of infringing domain names. To succeed, you must demonstrate that:
  ■ The domain name is identical or confusingly similar to your trademark.
  ■ The domain name owner has no legitimate interests or rights in the name.
  ■ The domain name was registered and is being used in bad faith.
o **URS**: The URS is a faster and less costly alternative to the UDRP, designed for clear-cut cases of cybersquatting. It allows trademark owners to suspend, but not transfer, infringing domain names.

- **Consider Legal Action**: In cases where UDRP or URS proceedings are unsuccessful, or if damages are substantial, you may consider filing a lawsuit under the Anti-Cybersquatting Consumer Protection Act (ACPA) or other applicable laws.

Protecting Trademarks Online

1. **Register Trademarks with the U.S. Patent and Trademark Office (USPTO)**

To strengthen your legal position and enhance your ability to protect your trademark online:

- **Federal Registration**: Register your trademarks with the USPTO to obtain nationwide protection and the right to use the ® symbol. This also provides a legal basis for challenging domain names that infringe on your trademark.
- **International Registration**: If you operate globally, consider registering your trademarks internationally through the Madrid System, managed by the World Intellectual Property Organization (WIPO). This system allows you to register trademarks in multiple countries with a single application.

2. **Use Trademark Notices and Symbols Online**

Prominently display trademark notices and symbols on your website and digital content to assert your rights and deter potential infringers:

- **Use the ® Symbol**: Display the ® symbol next to federally registered trademarks to indicate that your mark is protected by federal law.
- **Use the ™ Symbol**: Use the ™ symbol next to unregistered trademarks or common law marks to assert your claim to the mark.
- **Include Copyright Notices**: Include a copyright notice on all website content to indicate ownership and discourage unauthorized use.

3. Implement Trademark Monitoring and Enforcement Programs

Proactive monitoring and enforcement are crucial to protect your trademark online:

- **Monitor Online Marketplaces**: Regularly check online marketplaces (e.g., Amazon, eBay, Etsy) for unauthorized use of your trademarks. Many platforms offer brand protection programs to help trademark owners report and remove infringing listings.
- **Monitor Social Media**: Monitor social media platforms for misuse of your trademarks, such as counterfeit products, impersonation accounts, or unauthorized marketing campaigns. Report infringing accounts or content to the platform's legal or IP enforcement team.
- **Use Anti-Counterfeiting Tools**: Utilize tools and services that help identify and remove counterfeit products and infringing content, such as Amazon Brand Registry, eBay's Verified Rights Owner (VeRO) Program, and social media brand protection services.

4. Establish Clear Usage Guidelines

Provide clear guidelines for how your trademarks can be used by partners, affiliates, licensees, and other third parties:

- **Trademark Use Policy**: Develop a trademark use policy that outlines acceptable and unacceptable uses of your trademarks.

This policy should be shared with employees, partners, licensees, and affiliates.

- **License Agreements**: Include specific provisions in license agreements that regulate the use of your trademarks, including quality control measures, brand consistency requirements, and termination clauses for misuse.

5. **Prepare for and Address Trademark Disputes Online**

Be prepared to address trademark disputes quickly and efficiently:

- **Develop a Response Plan**: Create a response plan for handling online trademark disputes, including identifying key team members, legal counsel, and escalation procedures.
- **Resolve Disputes Amicably**: Whenever possible, try to resolve disputes amicably through negotiation or mediation before resorting to formal legal action. This can save time, money, and preserve business relationships.
- **File UDRP or ACPA Actions**: If amicable resolution fails, use UDRP proceedings or file a lawsuit under the ACPA to enforce your rights and recover damages.

Addressing Digital Infringements

Digital infringements, such as unauthorized use of copyrighted materials, trademark violations, and the distribution of counterfeit goods, are common challenges faced by IP owners in the online environment. To protect their rights, IP owners must adopt a proactive approach that includes monitoring the internet for potential violations and responding promptly and effectively to identified infringements.

Tools and Techniques for Monitoring and Responding to Online Violations

1. Use Digital Monitoring Tools to Detect Infringements

Monitoring tools play a crucial role in identifying unauthorized use of IP across websites, social media platforms, online marketplaces, and other digital channels. Several types of tools and services are available to help IP owners detect potential infringements:

- **Automated Web Crawlers and Search Engines**:

  Automated web crawlers, also known as web scrapers or bots, can continuously scan the internet to identify potential infringements. These tools search for specific keywords, phrases, trademarks, images, or other identifiers associated with your IP. Some of the popular web monitoring tools include:

  - **Google Alerts**: Set up Google Alerts for specific terms, such as your brand name, product name, or key trademarks. Alerts will notify you whenever these terms are mentioned on websites or blogs.
  - **Mention and Brandwatch**: These tools provide real-time alerts and comprehensive analytics for mentions of your brand or IP across various online platforms, including social media, forums, and blogs.
  - **Visualping**: Use tools like Visualping to monitor specific web pages for changes, such as unauthorized content appearing on a competitor's website.

- **Reverse Image Search Tools**:

  Reverse image search tools allow you to search for unauthorized use of your images, logos, or photographs:

  - **Google Reverse Image Search**: Upload an image or provide a URL to find where the image appears online. This is useful for detecting unauthorized use of copyrighted images or logos.
  - **TinEye**: A reverse image search engine that helps track the usage of your images across the web. TinEye also provides insights into how the image has been used, modified, or repurposed.

- **Digital Fingerprinting and Content ID Systems**:

  Digital fingerprinting technology assigns a unique digital "fingerprint" to each piece of content, such as an audio file, video, or image. These fingerprints can be used to identify and remove unauthorized copies:

- o **YouTube Content ID**: A tool for copyright owners to identify and manage their content on YouTube. Content ID scans videos uploaded to the platform and automatically detects matches against copyrighted content. Copyright owners can choose to monetize, block, or track videos that contain their content.
- o **Shazam for Brands**: This tool monitors audio content to identify unauthorized use of music tracks or sound recordings.

- **Social Media Monitoring Tools**:

  Social media platforms are often used to share content that may infringe on IP rights. Social media monitoring tools can help track unauthorized use:

  - o **Hootsuite, Sprout Social, and Meltwater**: These tools provide real-time monitoring and alerts for mentions of your brand, product names, or trademarks on social media platforms like Facebook, Twitter, Instagram, and LinkedIn.

- **Domain Monitoring Services**:

  Domain monitoring services help identify domain names that infringe on your trademark or brand:

  - o **DomainTools, MarkMonitor, and WhoisGuard**: These services monitor newly registered domain names that contain your brand name or trademarks. They provide alerts and reports, allowing you to act quickly against potential cybersquatters or infringers.

2. Respond to Infringements Using Takedown Procedures

Once an infringement is detected, it is essential to act promptly to mitigate damage. Several strategies and procedures can help address online violations:

- **Send a Cease and Desist Letter**:
  A cease and desist letter is a formal notice sent to the alleged infringer, demanding that they stop the unauthorized use of your IP. This letter typically includes:

- A description of the IP being infringed.
- Evidence of your ownership of the IP.
- A demand to cease the infringing activity.
- A deadline for compliance and a warning of potential legal action if the infringement continues.

- **File a DMCA Takedown Notice**:

The Digital Millennium Copyright Act (DMCA) provides a mechanism for copyright owners to request the removal of infringing content from websites, search engines, and platforms:

- **Prepare a Takedown Notice**: A DMCA takedown notice should include a description of the copyrighted work, the location (URL) of the infringing content, a statement of good faith belief that the use is unauthorized, and your contact information.
- **Send the Notice**: Submit the takedown notice to the hosting provider, website administrator, or platform (e.g., Google, YouTube) where the infringement is occurring.
- **Monitor Compliance**: After submitting the notice, monitor the situation to ensure that the infringing content is removed. Follow up with the service provider if necessary.

- **Use Platform-Specific IP Enforcement Tools**:

Many online platforms offer tools and procedures for reporting and addressing IP violations:

- **Amazon Brand Registry**: A program that helps brand owners protect their IP on Amazon by providing tools for reporting counterfeit products and unauthorized listings.
- **eBay Verified Rights Owner (VeRO) Program**: A program that enables rights owners to report listings that infringe on their IP rights.
- **Social Media Reporting Tools**: Most social media platforms, such as Facebook, Instagram, and Twitter, have dedicated tools for reporting content that infringes on copyrights, trademarks, or other IP rights.

- **Consider Legal Action for Persistent Infringement**:

  If other measures fail or the infringement is severe, legal action may be necessary:

  o **File a Lawsuit**: Consider filing a lawsuit in federal court to seek damages, injunctive relief, or other remedies. This is often appropriate for cases involving repeat offenders, significant financial losses, or reputational damage.
  o **Pursue Anti-Cybersquatting Remedies**: If the infringement involves a domain name, consider filing a complaint under the Uniform Domain-Name Dispute-Resolution Policy (UDRP) or a lawsuit under the Anti-Cybersquatting Consumer Protection Act (ACPA).

3. Engage in Negotiation and Alternative Dispute Resolution (ADR)

Before resorting to litigation, consider negotiation or alternative dispute resolution (ADR) methods to settle the dispute amicably:

- **Direct Negotiation**: Contact the infringer directly to negotiate a resolution. This may involve reaching a licensing agreement, settlement, or other mutually beneficial arrangements.
- **Mediation**: Use mediation, where a neutral third party facilitates negotiations between the disputing parties to reach a mutually acceptable solution. Mediation is confidential, cost-effective, and can preserve business relationships.
- **Arbitration**: Opt for arbitration, where an arbitrator reviews the evidence and makes a binding decision. Arbitration can be faster and less expensive than litigation, providing a more structured process for resolving disputes.

4. Maintain an Infringement Response Plan

An infringement response plan outlines the steps to be taken when an infringement is detected. It ensures that the organization can act quickly and consistently to protect its IP:

- **Create a Response Team**: Designate a response team that includes members from legal, marketing, and IT departments.

Assign specific roles and responsibilities for handling infringement cases.

- **Develop a Takedown Template Library**: Prepare templates for cease and desist letters, DMCA notices, and other takedown requests to streamline the response process.
- **Establish Response Timelines**: Set clear timelines for detecting, investigating, and responding to infringements. Quick response times are essential for minimizing damage and deterring future infringements.
- **Document Actions Taken**: Keep detailed records of all actions taken to address each infringement, including correspondence, takedown notices, and legal actions. This documentation can serve as evidence in future disputes and demonstrates due diligence.

5. Leverage Technology and Partnerships for IP Protection

Technology and partnerships can enhance your ability to monitor and respond to digital infringements:

- **Use AI and Machine Learning Tools**: Employ artificial intelligence (AI) and machine learning tools to automate the detection of infringing content. These tools can analyze vast amounts of data, identify patterns, and flag potential violations more efficiently than manual monitoring.
- **Collaborate with Industry Partners**: Work with industry organizations, trade groups, and IP enforcement agencies to share information, coordinate actions, and strengthen collective efforts against digital infringements.
- **Engage Professional Services**: Consider hiring specialized IP enforcement firms or legal experts who can provide advanced monitoring services, assist in responding to complex cases, and represent your interests in legal proceedings.

Chapter 7:

Sustaining and Monitoring Intellectual Property Rights in the United States

This chapter focuses on the ongoing maintenance of intellectual property (IP) rights to ensure they remain valid, enforceable, and effectively protected. It covers the strategies and techniques necessary for monitoring potential infringements and renewing rights to maintain a robust IP portfolio.

Monitoring IP Infringements and Renewing Rights (4-5 pages)

Maintaining IP rights is an active process that requires regular monitoring for potential infringements, timely renewal of registrations, and proactive enforcement to protect against unauthorized use. This section outlines key techniques for keeping IP rights current and protected, enabling businesses to maximize the value of their IP assets and avoid loss or weakening of rights.

Techniques for Keeping IP Rights Current and Protected

1. Regularly Monitor for IP Infringements

Monitoring for potential infringements is essential to detect unauthorized use of your IP promptly and to take appropriate action to prevent damage. Effective monitoring involves using a combination of tools and strategies to cover all possible sources of infringement:

- **Conduct Routine Searches**: Perform regular searches for your trademarks, copyrights, and patents across various platforms:
  - **Trademark Searches**: Use trademark search databases such as the United States Patent and Trademark Office (USPTO) Trademark Electronic Search System (TESS) and international databases like the World Intellectual Property Organization (WIPO) Global Brand Database to find similar or conflicting marks.

- o **Patent Searches**: Regularly check patent databases, such as the USPTO Patent Full-Text and Image Database (PatFT), to identify potentially infringing patents or applications.
- o **Copyright Searches**: Monitor platforms where your copyrighted content could be shared, such as stock photo sites, video-sharing platforms, and social media networks. Use reverse image search tools like Google Images and TinEye to find unauthorized use of visual content.

- **Leverage Automated Monitoring Tools**: Utilize automated tools and services that continuously scan the web for potential infringements:

  - o **Web Crawlers**: Deploy web crawlers that search for unauthorized use of your trademarks, copyrighted materials, or patents. Tools like Mention, Brand24, and Ahrefs can track mentions of your brand or IP across websites, blogs, and forums.
  - o **Reverse Image and Audio Search Tools**: Use reverse image search tools like Google Reverse Image Search or TinEye to find unauthorized uses of your images or logos. Employ digital audio fingerprinting tools like Shazam for Brands to identify unauthorized use of audio content.
  - o **Social Media Monitoring**: Use social media monitoring tools like Hootsuite or Sprout Social to track mentions of your brand or IP on social networks. Report infringing content to the platform's legal or IP enforcement team as needed.

- **Monitor Competitors and Industry Developments**: Keep an eye on competitors' activities and developments within your industry:

  - o **Competitor Analysis**: Regularly review competitors' websites, products, and marketing materials to detect any potential infringement of your IP. Look for similar branding, product designs, or technology.
  - o **Industry Reports and Publications**: Subscribe to industry reports, newsletters, and trade publications to stay informed

about new market entrants, product launches, and emerging trends that could impact your IP.

2. Develop an IP Renewal Calendar

Timely renewal of IP rights is critical to maintaining their validity and enforceability. Different types of IP have different renewal requirements and timelines, making it essential to keep track of renewal deadlines:

- **Create a Renewal Schedule**: Develop a comprehensive IP renewal schedule that lists all your IP assets and their respective renewal deadlines:
  - **Trademarks**: In the United States, trademarks must be renewed between the fifth and sixth year after registration, and again between the ninth and tenth year. Subsequent renewals are required every ten years thereafter.
  - **Patents**: Utility patents in the U.S. require maintenance fees at 3.5, 7.5, and 11.5 years after grant. Design patents do not require maintenance fees but expire 15 years from the grant date.
  - **Copyrights**: Copyrights do not require formal renewals but monitoring unauthorized use is essential to prevent infringement.
- **Use IP Management Software**: Consider using IP management software, such as CPA Global or Anaqua, to automate and track renewal deadlines, manage documents, and receive alerts for upcoming renewal dates.
- **Assign Responsibility for Renewals**: Designate a specific person or team within your organization to be responsible for tracking, managing, and executing IP renewals. This ensures accountability and reduces the risk of missing important deadlines.

3. Keep IP Documentation Updated and Organized

Proper documentation is crucial for demonstrating ownership, maintaining rights, and enforcing IP in disputes. Regularly review and update all IP-related documentation to ensure it is complete, accurate, and easily accessible:

- **Maintain Accurate Records of Registrations and Renewals**: Keep a well-organized database of all IP registrations, certificates, renewal applications, and related documents. Include details such as registration numbers, filing dates, expiration dates, and renewal statuses.
- **Document Use and Enforcement Actions**: For trademarks, maintain records of how the mark is used in commerce, including packaging, advertising, and sales data. Document any enforcement actions taken, such as cease and desist letters or DMCA takedown notices, to establish a record of defending your rights.
- **Centralize IP Information**: Use a centralized IP management system or database to store and organize all IP-related documents, including licenses, assignments, contracts, and legal correspondence. Ensure access is restricted to authorized personnel to maintain confidentiality and security.

4. Review and Update Licensing Agreements Regularly

Licensing agreements are a valuable way to monetize IP, but they must be actively managed to ensure compliance and maximize revenue:

- **Conduct Regular Audits of Licensees**: Periodically review licensee activities to ensure they are complying with the terms of the license agreement. Check that royalties are being paid accurately and on time, and that the IP is being used within the agreed scope.
- **Update Agreements to Reflect Changes**: If there are changes in the market, law, or your business strategy, update existing licensing agreements to reflect new terms or conditions. For example, consider including clauses that account for new digital distribution methods or emerging technologies.
- **Include Renewal and Termination Clauses**: Ensure that all licensing agreements include clear terms for renewal and termination. Specify the duration of the agreement, the conditions under which it can be renewed, and any actions required for renewal.

5. Enforce IP Rights Proactively

Proactive enforcement is necessary to maintain the value and exclusivity of your IP rights. When infringements occur, act quickly to assert your rights and prevent further unauthorized use:

- **Send Cease and Desist Letters**: As soon as an infringement is detected, send a cease and desist letter to the infringer. Clearly state your rights, describe the unauthorized activity, and demand that the infringer stop the activity and take corrective actions. This often serves as a first step before pursuing more formal legal action.

- **Use Takedown Procedures**: For online infringements, use takedown procedures such as DMCA notices or platform-specific reporting tools to remove infringing content from websites, social media platforms, or online marketplaces.

- **File Lawsuits When Necessary**: In cases of significant infringement or when other remedies fail, consider filing a lawsuit to enforce your rights. Seek remedies such as damages, injunctions, or court orders to stop the infringing activity.

- **Collaborate with Enforcement Agencies**: Work with law enforcement agencies, customs authorities, and industry organizations to identify and prevent IP theft, counterfeiting, or piracy. Use partnerships to enhance enforcement capabilities and share information on known infringers.

6. Stay Informed About Legal Changes and Best Practices

IP laws and regulations are constantly evolving, and staying informed is essential for maintaining effective IP protection strategies:

- **Monitor Changes in IP Laws**: Keep track of changes in U.S. IP laws, international treaties, and court rulings that could affect your rights. Follow updates from the USPTO, WIPO, and relevant trade organizations.

- **Participate in IP Forums and Associations**: Join IP associations, forums, and industry groups to stay connected with other IP professionals and learn about new best practices, tools, and trends.

- **Engage IP Legal Experts**: Consult with IP attorneys regularly to review your IP portfolio, ensure compliance with legal requirements, and update strategies in response to changing laws or market conditions.

Tools and Resources for Ongoing Monitoring

Monitoring IP is an ongoing process that requires specialized tools and services to identify unauthorized use, detect potential infringements, and manage enforcement actions. There are various software solutions and monitoring services available that cater to different types of IP—such as trademarks, patents, and copyrights—across different platforms and media.

Software Solutions and Services for IP Monitoring

1. Trademark Monitoring Tools

Trademarks are valuable assets that help build brand recognition and consumer trust. To protect trademarks effectively, businesses must monitor for potential infringements that could dilute their brand or cause consumer confusion. Several software solutions and services offer comprehensive trademark monitoring capabilities:

- **Trademark Watch Services**:

  These services monitor trademark databases, business directories, domain names, and online content for potential trademark infringements:

  o **Corsearch**: Provides global trademark search and watch services, monitoring trademarks, company names, domain names, and online content. Corsearch also offers automated alerts and in-depth analytics to help trademark owners respond to potential infringements.
  o **CompuMark**: Offers trademark monitoring services that cover various jurisdictions worldwide. CompuMark monitors new trademark applications, domain name registrations, and online use of similar or identical marks. It provides customizable watch reports and actionable insights.

140

- o **TrademarkNow**: An AI-powered trademark search and monitoring platform that offers real-time monitoring of trademark applications and registrations. TrademarkNow's algorithms analyze trademark databases and online content to detect potentially conflicting marks.

- **Domain Name Monitoring**:

  Domain name monitoring services help detect unauthorized domain registrations that could infringe on your trademark:

  - o **MarkMonitor**: A domain name management and brand protection service that monitors domain registrations globally. MarkMonitor provides alerts when similar domain names are registered and offers recovery services to help secure infringing domains.
  - o **DomainTools**: Tracks domain name registrations and monitors changes in domain ownership or configuration that could indicate cybersquatting or other unauthorized activities. DomainTools also provides detailed reports and analytics on domain activity.

2. Patent Monitoring Tools

Patent monitoring is essential for identifying potential patent infringements, tracking competitor activities, and staying informed about technological advancements. Patent monitoring tools help patent owners maintain a competitive edge by detecting new patents, applications, and related technologies that could impact their IP rights:

- **Patent Search and Monitoring Databases**:

  These tools provide access to global patent databases and enable automated monitoring of new patent filings and publications:

  - o **Questel Orbit**: A comprehensive patent search and monitoring platform that offers global coverage of patent databases. Questel Orbit allows users to set up alerts for new patents, applications, and changes to existing patents in specific technical fields or jurisdictions.

- Derwent Innovation (Clarivate Analytics): A patent research and analytics platform that provides access to over 90 million patent records worldwide. Derwent Innovation offers monitoring services that track patent applications, grants, and legal status changes, along with in-depth analysis of competitor patent portfolios.
- PatentSight: A patent analytics and monitoring tool that focuses on patent quality and competitive positioning. PatentSight provides insights into patent strength, market value, and infringement risk through its proprietary scoring models.

- **Patent Alert Services**:

  Patent alert services notify patent owners of new patent applications, grants, and legal changes that may impact their IP rights:

  - Google Patents: Allows users to create alerts for specific keywords, inventors, assignees, or classifications. Google Patents sends email notifications when new patents or applications matching the criteria are published.
  - USPTO Alerts: The United States Patent and Trademark Office (USPTO) offers email alert services for specific patents or applications. Users can subscribe to receive notifications on prosecution events, status changes, and other updates.

3. Copyright Monitoring Tools

Copyright monitoring is essential for detecting unauthorized use of creative works, such as images, videos, music, software, and written content. Several tools and services help copyright owners protect their works across various digital platforms:

- **Digital Content Identification and Monitoring**:

  These tools use advanced algorithms, digital fingerprinting, and content recognition technologies to detect and manage copyright violations:

o **YouTube Content ID**: A content recognition system for identifying copyrighted audio and video on YouTube. Copyright owners can upload reference files, and YouTube scans new uploads to find matches. Owners can choose to monetize, block, or track infringing content.

o **Pixsy**: An image monitoring and enforcement service that uses reverse image search technology to detect unauthorized use of photographs and images across the web. Pixsy provides tools for sending takedown notices, negotiating settlements, or pursuing legal action.

o **Copytrack**: A copyright monitoring and enforcement service that helps photographers, artists, and content creators detect and address unauthorized use of their work online. Copytrack offers automated detection and provides support for settlement negotiations or litigation.

- **Text and Content Monitoring Tools**:

These tools help detect plagiarism, unauthorized reproduction, and other forms of copyright infringement related to text-based content:

o **Copyscape**: An online plagiarism detection tool that scans the web for copies of your text content. Copyscape provides a detailed report of duplicate content and offers options for addressing infringements.

o **Plagscan**: A plagiarism checker that detects copied content across websites, academic papers, and online publications. Plagscan provides a similarity score and highlights potential matches for further investigation.

4. Social Media Monitoring Tools

Social media is a common platform for unauthorized use of IP, including counterfeit sales, brand impersonation, and unauthorized content distribution. Monitoring tools can help track IP use on social networks:

- **Social Media Management Platforms**:
These platforms offer brand monitoring, sentiment analysis, and IP protection capabilities:

143

- o **Hootsuite**: A social media management tool that monitors multiple social networks for brand mentions, hashtags, and keywords. Hootsuite allows users to track unauthorized content, identify impersonation accounts, and report violations directly to the platform.
- o **Sprout Social**: Provides social listening and brand monitoring capabilities, enabling users to track brand mentions, comments, and content across social networks. Sprout Social offers customizable alerts and reporting features.
- o **Brandwatch**: A social media analytics platform that monitors online conversations, mentions, and sentiment related to your brand. Brandwatch can track IP violations, counterfeit sales, and unauthorized content sharing across social networks and forums.

5. Comprehensive IP Management Platforms

Comprehensive IP management platforms provide end-to-end solutions for monitoring, protecting, and managing IP portfolios. These platforms integrate various tools and services to offer centralized management, reporting, and enforcement capabilities:

- **Anaqua**: An IP management software that offers a suite of tools for trademark, patent, and copyright monitoring, as well as portfolio management, IP strategy, and analytics. Anaqua provides customizable dashboards, automated alerts, and workflow automation to streamline IP management processes.
- **CPA Global**: A cloud-based IP management platform that provides tools for monitoring trademarks, patents, and copyrights, along with renewal management, IP valuation, and analytics. CPA Global offers automated alerts, detailed reports, and collaboration features to help IP owners maintain control over their assets.
- **PatSnap**: An IP intelligence platform that combines patent, trademark, and copyright monitoring with data analytics, competitive intelligence, and innovation tracking. PatSnap

provides visualizations, alerts, and detailed reports to help businesses make data-driven decisions about their IP strategy.

6. Engaging Professional IP Monitoring Services

For businesses with large or complex IP portfolios, engaging professional IP monitoring services can offer added expertise and resources:

- **IP Law Firms and Agencies**: Many law firms and specialized IP agencies offer monitoring services that include regular searches, watch reports, and enforcement support. These professionals can provide tailored advice and representation in complex infringement cases.
- **Brand Protection Companies**: Companies like OpSec Security, Red Points, and Yellow Brand Protection provide comprehensive brand protection services, including online monitoring, anti-counterfeiting measures, and enforcement actions.

Staying Informed About Legal Changes

Keeping current with IP laws and regulations is crucial for businesses and individuals to protect their IP assets, avoid legal risks, and make informed decisions. This section provides a list of valuable resources and methods to stay informed about regulatory changes affecting IP in the United States and globally.

Resources for Keeping Updated on Regulatory Developments

1. Government and Official Websites

Government websites are primary sources of information on current laws, proposed legislation, and regulatory updates. These sites offer access to legal texts, official notices, guidelines, and public consultations:

- **United States Patent and Trademark Office (USPTO)**:

    The USPTO website is an essential resource for updates on U.S. patent and trademark laws, regulations, and policies:

- **News and Updates**: Regularly check the USPTO's news section for announcements about rule changes, fee adjustments, and policy updates.
- **Official Gazette**: Subscribe to the USPTO's Official Gazette, a weekly publication that lists new trademarks, patents, and other IP-related decisions.
- **USPTO Blog**: Follow the USPTO blog for insights on recent developments, changes in procedures, and explanations of new regulations.
- **USPTO Events and Webinars**: Participate in USPTO-hosted events, webinars, and public hearings to learn about regulatory changes and best practices directly from experts and policymakers.

- **U.S. Copyright Office**:

The U.S. Copyright Office provides resources and updates on copyright law and policy in the United States:

- **News and Announcements**: Check the U.S. Copyright Office's news section for updates on legislative changes, policy statements, and procedural amendments.
- **Public Notices and Reports**: Access public notices, reports, and studies on topics such as digital copyright issues, orphan works, and licensing.
- **Webinars and Events**: Attend webinars, workshops, and public events hosted by the U.S. Copyright Office to stay informed about current copyright issues and future legislative changes.

- **World Intellectual Property Organization (WIPO)**:

WIPO is a global organization dedicated to promoting IP protection and harmonization across different jurisdictions:

- **WIPO Lex**: Use WIPO Lex, an online database of national IP laws, treaties, and regulations from member countries worldwide. It provides access to the full texts of IP legislation, judicial decisions, and regulatory updates.

- o **WIPO News**: Follow WIPO News for updates on global IP developments, international agreements, and conferences.
- o **Webinars and Online Training**: Participate in WIPO's webinars, online courses, and training sessions to gain insights into international IP issues and legal changes.

2. Legal Databases and Research Tools

Legal databases provide access to a wide range of legal materials, including case law, statutes, regulations, and secondary sources that offer insights into recent IP developments:

- **Westlaw and LexisNexis**:

  These comprehensive legal research platforms provide access to U.S. and international case law, statutes, administrative rules, and legal commentary. Use Westlaw and LexisNexis to:

  - o Track changes in IP laws and regulations.
  - o Review recent court decisions that may impact IP rights.
  - o Access legal articles, journals, and treatises on emerging IP topics.

- **Bloomberg Law**:

  Bloomberg Law offers a specialized IP practice center with news, analysis, and primary legal sources. It includes:

  - o Real-time updates on IP litigation and regulatory developments.
  - o Access to the latest court opinions, agency decisions, and regulatory filings.
  - o Expert commentary and analysis from leading IP practitioners and scholars.

- **Justia and FindLaw**:

  Free legal research websites that provide access to U.S. laws, regulations, and court decisions. Use Justia and FindLaw to:

  - o Monitor recent rulings and legislative changes in IP law.
  - o Search for IP-related statutes and regulations.

o Access legal blogs, newsletters, and forums to stay updated on current trends and discussions.

3. Industry Associations and Professional Organizations

Joining industry associations and professional organizations provides access to a network of IP professionals, thought leaders, and policymakers who share insights and updates on legal changes:

- **International Trademark Association (INTA)**:

  INTA is a global organization focused on trademark law and practice. Benefits of membership include:

  o Access to daily and weekly newsletters that cover global trademark developments and legislative updates.
  o Participation in conferences, webinars, and roundtables on trademark law and policy.
  o Networking opportunities with other IP professionals and access to specialized committees on specific trademark issues.

- **American Intellectual Property Law Association (AIPLA)**:

  AIPLA represents IP lawyers and professionals in the United States. Members can benefit from:

  o Newsletters, journals, and blogs that cover recent IP developments, court cases, and legislative changes.
  o Access to webinars, conferences, and training sessions on emerging IP issues.
  o Opportunities to join specialized committees focused on different aspects of IP law, such as patents, copyrights, and trademarks.

- **Intellectual Property Owners Association (IPO)**:

  IPO is an organization for companies and individuals involved in IP ownership and management. Membership provides:

  o Regular updates on legislative changes, policy developments, and court decisions.
  o Access to webinars, podcasts, and educational programs.

- Opportunities to participate in advocacy efforts, policy discussions, and networking events.

- **Licensing Executives Society (LES)**:

    LES is a professional organization for licensing professionals, patent holders, and technology transfer experts. Membership benefits include:

    - Access to news, articles, and resources on licensing, technology transfer, and IP monetization.
    - Participation in workshops, conferences, and training programs.
    - Networking with peers and experts in IP licensing and management.

4. IP Law Firms and Expert Blogs

Leading IP law firms and expert blogs provide timely commentary, analysis, and insights on changes in IP law:

- **Law Firm Newsletters and Blogs**:

    Many law firms publish newsletters, blogs, and alerts on IP law developments. Subscribe to newsletters from leading IP law firms like Finnegan, Fish & Richardson, and Quinn Emanuel to receive updates on:

    - Recent court rulings and case summaries.
    - Legislative and regulatory changes.
    - Emerging trends and best practices in IP protection.

- **Specialized IP Blogs**:

    Follow specialized IP blogs such as IPWatchdog, Patently-O, and The IPKat for in-depth analysis and commentary on IP news and trends. These blogs often cover breaking news, provide case summaries, and discuss the implications of regulatory changes.

5. Online Courses, Webinars, and Training Programs

Participating in online courses, webinars, and training programs can help you stay informed about legal changes and deepen your understanding of IP law:

- **Coursera, edX, and Udemy**:

  These platforms offer courses on IP law, including modules on recent developments, international treaties, and emerging issues. Many courses are taught by leading IP professionals, academics, and industry experts.

- **Bar Associations and Continuing Legal Education (CLE)**:

  State bar associations and other legal organizations offer CLE courses that cover recent changes in IP law, case law updates, and regulatory developments. CLE courses are an excellent way to stay current with legal changes and fulfill continuing education requirements.

6. News Outlets and Trade Publications

News outlets and trade publications provide timely news and analysis on IP developments and industry trends:

- **IPWatchdog and World IP Review**:

  Online publications that focus on IP news, trends, and policy changes. These resources offer breaking news, opinion pieces, interviews, and detailed analysis of important IP issues.

- **The Wall Street Journal, Bloomberg, and Reuters**:

  Major news outlets often report on significant IP-related developments, including high-profile court cases, regulatory changes, and industry trends. Regularly checking these sources can help you stay informed about important changes that may affect your IP rights.

Chapter 8:
AI-Generated Works and the Existing Legal Framework in the United States

Definition and Categories of AI-Generated Works

Legal Definition of AI-Generated Works: What They Are and How They Are Created

AI-generated works refer to creative outputs that are produced either entirely or partially through the use of artificial intelligence (AI) technologies. These works can include a variety of mediums such as text, visual art, music, video, and even software code. The legal definition of AI-generated works is currently evolving, as jurisdictions around the world seek to understand and regulate creations made by machines that simulate human intelligence.

Understanding AI-Generated Works

AI-generated works are typically the result of machine learning algorithms, neural networks, or other AI techniques that have been trained on large datasets to generate new content. This content can range from written articles and news reports to digital artworks and music compositions. For example, an AI can be trained on a vast corpus of existing literature to generate new stories or on a database of musical compositions to produce unique musical pieces. These outputs may be created autonomously by the AI or with varying degrees of human intervention.

Categories of AI-Generated Works

There are generally two main categories of AI-generated works:

- **AI-Assisted Works (Human-in-the-Loop):** In these cases, AI tools are used to assist human creators in the creative process. The AI may suggest ideas, provide tools for content creation, or automate certain aspects of the work, but the human retains a significant degree of control and authorship. An example could be a digital artist using AI-based software to generate patterns or textures that they incorporate into a final piece.

- **Fully Autonomous AI Works:** These are works created entirely by an AI system with no direct human involvement in the creative process. For instance, an AI algorithm that autonomously generates a piece of music or visual art without any input or guidance from a human would be considered a fully autonomous AI work. These works raise unique legal and ethical questions, especially concerning the ownership and authorship rights associated with them.

Legal Definitions and Challenges

The legal definition of AI-generated works is still under development and varies significantly across jurisdictions. In the United States, the current copyright law (under the Copyright Act of 1976) presumes that a human being must be the author of a work to claim copyright protection. This has led to legal challenges and debates over whether AI-generated works can be protected under existing intellectual property laws. Key issues include:

- **Authorship and Ownership:** Can an AI be considered an "author," or must the ownership of the work default to the human creator, programmer, or owner of the AI?
- **Originality and Creativity Requirements:** Do AI-generated works meet the requirements for originality and creativity as defined by copyright law? If the work lacks human creativity, it may not qualify for protection.
- **Legal Precedents and Cases:** Court cases, such as Thaler v. Copyright Office, have highlighted the challenges of defining authorship for AI-generated works. In this case, an AI-generated image was denied copyright protection because it did not have a human author.

Key Components of Legal Analysis for AI-Generated Works

When analyzing AI-generated works under current legal frameworks, several components must be considered:

- **Source of the Work:** Was the work created by a fully autonomous AI, or was it assisted by a human?
- **Level of Human Intervention:** What degree of human involvement was required in the creative process? This could affect whether the work is considered "authored" by a human and thus eligible for protection.
- **Nature of the Creative Process:** Understanding whether the AI generated the work through purely algorithmic means or if there was any element of decision-making or creativity that could be attributed to a human.
- **Existing Legal Frameworks and Interpretations:** Analyzing how existing copyright laws apply to works generated by non-human entities and how different jurisdictions are approaching this emerging issue.

Main Categories: Textual Works, Visual Art, Music, and Software Code

AI-generated works span a broad spectrum of creative outputs across various domains. Each category presents unique challenges and considerations regarding intellectual property rights and the existing legal framework.

Textual Works

Textual works generated by AI can include anything from articles, poems, and short stories to news reports, legal documents, and academic papers. These works are typically produced using natural language processing (NLP) algorithms, which are trained on large datasets of text to generate coherent and contextually relevant written content.

- **Creation Process:** AI-generated textual works are often produced by algorithms such as GPT (Generative Pre-trained Transformer) models, which can predict and generate text based on the input they receive. These models are trained on massive datasets, such as books, articles, and other written materials, enabling them to create original text that mimics human writing styles.

- **Legal Considerations:** Textual works generated by AI face specific legal challenges regarding copyright protection. Under current U.S. law, the Copyright Office has determined that textual content requires a "human author" to be eligible for copyright. This raises questions about the protection of content produced solely by machines, as it may not meet the originality and creativity standards required by the law. Additionally, concerns arise about potential copyright infringement if the AI uses copyrighted materials from its training data without permission.

Visual Art

AI-generated visual art encompasses various forms, including digital paintings, illustrations, photography, and design elements. These works are created using algorithms that analyze and replicate visual patterns, colors, and compositions.

- **Creation Process:** Visual art can be generated using deep learning models such as Generative Adversarial Networks (GANs), which consist of two neural networks: a generator and a discriminator. The generator creates new images based on training data, while the discriminator evaluates their authenticity. This iterative process allows the AI to produce visually appealing and sometimes highly complex artworks.
- **Legal Considerations:** For visual art, the primary legal issues concern authorship and originality. Since AI can generate images based on vast datasets that may include copyrighted works, determining whether the output is genuinely "original" or an infringement becomes complex. Furthermore, the question of whether an AI can hold copyright or if it should be attributed to the human developer or user of the AI remains unresolved.

Music

AI-generated music ranges from simple compositions to complex symphonies and is created using machine learning techniques that analyze patterns in musical structure, melody, harmony, and rhythm.

- **Creation Process:** AI can generate music using various techniques, including recurrent neural networks (RNNs), which are particularly suited for sequential data like music. These algorithms can learn the patterns of existing music and create new compositions that adhere to similar styles or innovate with new combinations of sounds and rhythms.
- **Legal Considerations:** The legal challenges for AI-generated music are multifaceted. Copyright law traditionally requires human creativity for protection, posing questions about the eligibility of music created solely by AI. Additionally, there is the issue of potential infringement if the AI-generated composition is too similar to existing works, especially if it was trained on copyrighted music. This can lead to legal disputes over whether the new piece is sufficiently original or derivative.

Software Code

AI-generated software code refers to code produced by machine learning algorithms, often to perform specific functions or solve particular problems.

- **Creation Process:** AI can generate software code through techniques like program synthesis, where the AI system creates code based on a given set of requirements or specifications. Additionally, some AI models, such as Codex, are trained on large datasets of existing code to assist developers by auto-completing code, suggesting functions, or even writing entire programs.
- **Legal Considerations:** The creation of software code by AI introduces unique legal challenges. While software is generally considered a "literary work" under copyright law, questions arise regarding who owns the rights to code generated autonomously by AI. If an AI creates code that performs a specific patented function, the ownership and infringement issues become even more complicated. Moreover, if AI-generated code uses existing codebases or libraries, there could be potential copyright violations or issues related to open-source licensing.

Distinguishing Between AI-Assisted (Human-in-the-Loop) and Fully Autonomous Works: Legal Criteria

Understanding the distinction between AI-assisted (Human-in-the-Loop) and fully autonomous AI-generated works is crucial in determining how intellectual property laws apply to these creations.

AI-Assisted (Human-in-the-Loop) Works

AI-assisted works involve a collaborative process between a human creator and an AI tool. In this model, the AI acts as an aid or tool to enhance the human's creative process, but the human retains significant control and authorship over the final output.

- **Definition and Examples:** AI-assisted works are those where the human uses AI tools to facilitate the creation but maintains creative oversight. For example, an author might use an AI writing assistant to suggest plot points or generate dialogue, but the overall storyline, characters, and writing style are determined by the human author. Similarly, a graphic designer might use an AI to generate patterns or textures but integrates them into a larger design that reflects their creative vision.
- **Legal Implications:** In cases of AI-assisted works, the human is generally recognized as the author and retains the copyright since they provide the creative input and decision-making. The AI is viewed as a tool, much like a camera or a paintbrush, used to achieve the desired result. The legal criteria for authorship and ownership remain relatively straightforward under current intellectual property laws, which prioritize human creativity and intention.

Fully Autonomous AI Works

Fully autonomous AI works are created without any direct human intervention in the creative process. The AI system independently generates the output based on its training and programming.

- **Definition and Examples:** Fully autonomous works are those where the AI operates independently, creating a work without specific human guidance or input. For example, an AI trained on thousands of musical compositions might independently compose a new symphony without any human involvement in the creation process. Similarly, an AI model might generate a visual artwork or write a piece of literature entirely on its own, based on patterns it has learned from its training data.

- **Legal Implications:** Fully autonomous works raise complex legal questions, as traditional intellectual property laws do not recognize machines or software as "authors." The key legal issues include:
  - o **Authorship:** Current laws generally require a human creator for copyright protection, which may exclude fully autonomous works from copyright eligibility.
  - o **Ownership:** If the work cannot be attributed to a human author, there is no clear guidance on who owns the rights to such works. Possibilities include the developer of the AI, the user who commissioned the work, or even the owner of the dataset used to train the AI.
  - o **Originality and Creativity:** Fully autonomous AI works may struggle to meet the legal standards for originality and creativity, as they lack human authorship. Courts may need to develop new criteria to assess these works.

Key Legal Criteria for Distinction

The distinction between AI-assisted and fully autonomous works is critical in applying intellectual property laws. Key criteria include:

- **Degree of Human Involvement:** Assessing how much control or influence a human had in the creation process.
- **Nature of AI's Role:** Determining whether the AI acted as a mere tool or was the primary creator of the work.
- **Intent and Creativity:** Evaluating whether human creativity, intent, and originality are present in the final product.

By understanding these distinctions, legal frameworks can better address the complexities of AI-generated works and ensure appropriate protection and recognition under intellectual property laws.

The Current Legal Framework in the United States

Intellectual Property of Machine-Generated Works: Current Status and Lack of Specific Regulation

AI-generated works present novel challenges for the existing intellectual property (IP) framework in the United States, primarily because current laws were not designed with the capabilities of artificial intelligence in mind. The U.S. legal system is built around the notion of human authorship and originality, both of which become complicated when dealing with works produced by machines. This section explores the current status of IP protection for machine-generated works and highlights the gaps and ambiguities in the regulatory framework.

Current Legal Stance on AI-Generated Works

As of now, the United States does not have specific legislation that directly addresses the intellectual property status of AI-generated works. Existing IP laws, such as the Copyright Act of 1976, the Patent Act, and the Lanham Act, are grounded in the assumption that only human beings can be authors or inventors. These laws provide protections for human creativity and ingenuity, but they do not explicitly contemplate creations produced by machines.

- **Copyright Law:** According to the U.S. Copyright Office, works must have a human author to qualify for copyright protection. The office's Compendium of U.S. Copyright Office Practices explicitly states that "works produced by a machine or mere mechanical process that operates randomly or automatically without any creative input or intervention from a human author are not registrable." This effectively excludes fully autonomous AI-generated works from copyright protection. Recent cases, such as the Thaler v. Copyright Office, have reinforced this position by denying copyright registration to AI-generated content on the grounds that it lacks human authorship.
- **Patent Law:** The U.S. Patent and Trademark Office (USPTO) currently only grants patents to human inventors. A patent must be filed in the name of a natural person, which excludes AI systems from being recognized as inventors. This position was

confirmed in a 2020 decision where the USPTO rejected patent applications listing an AI as the inventor. The USPTO emphasized that, under current law, only human beings are considered eligible inventors. This interpretation has raised concerns about how inventions created entirely by AI or with substantial AI involvement can be protected.

- **Trademark Law:** Trademark law in the U.S., governed by the Lanham Act, is also built around the concept of human use in commerce. Trademarks are generally understood as symbols, names, or designs used by businesses or individuals to distinguish their goods and services. While trademarks could theoretically be generated by AI, the application of trademark law to AI-generated marks is still unclear, especially regarding who would own the rights to such marks and how they would be enforced.

Lack of Specific Regulation and Emerging Gaps

The absence of specific regulations addressing AI-generated works has led to significant gaps and uncertainties in the current legal landscape:

- **Unclear Ownership and Authorship:** Since existing laws require human authorship for copyright and patent protection, there is no clear legal path for protecting works created solely by AI. This ambiguity raises questions about who, if anyone, can claim ownership of AI-generated works. Possibilities include the developer of the AI, the user who operates the AI, or the entity that owns the data used to train the AI.
- **Lack of Precedent for AI-Generated IP Disputes:** Few legal precedents exist to guide courts in disputes over AI-generated works. While some cases have begun to address these issues, such as the aforementioned Thaler case, there is still a lack of comprehensive case law that offers clear guidance on how to handle such disputes. This creates uncertainty for creators, businesses, and legal practitioners.
- **Challenges to the Principle of Originality:** Traditional IP law relies on the concept of originality, which is typically associated with human creativity and effort. AI-generated works, especially

159

those created autonomously by machines, may challenge this principle, as the "creativity" involved does not originate from a human mind. As a result, there is a lack of consensus on whether such works meet the criteria for originality required for IP protection.

- **Inadequate Frameworks for Determining Liability:** In cases where AI-generated works infringe upon existing IP rights or cause other legal harms, there is no established framework for determining liability. Questions arise about whether the developer, user, or owner of the AI should be held accountable, and under what circumstances. The absence of clear regulations and guidelines creates a legal gray area, complicating enforcement and dispute resolution.

Key Issues and Considerations for Future Regulation

Given the current lack of specific regulation, several key issues must be considered to develop a more comprehensive legal framework for AI-generated works:

- **Revising Definitions of Authorship and Inventorship:** To accommodate AI-generated works, lawmakers may need to revise existing definitions of authorship and inventorship to consider non-human entities or to attribute rights to the parties most closely associated with the creation process (e.g., developers, operators, or data owners).
- **Developing New Legal Categories or Protections:** Another potential approach is to create new categories or forms of protection specifically tailored for AI-generated works. For example, a distinct category for "machine-generated works" could be established, with its own set of rules governing ownership, rights, and enforcement.
- **Creating Clear Guidelines for Liability and Enforcement:** As AI-generated works become more prevalent, it will be crucial to establish clear guidelines for determining liability in cases of IP infringement or other legal violations. This may involve developing new legal doctrines or adapting existing ones to account for the unique characteristics of AI-generated content.

160

- **International Harmonization:** Since AI-generated works can easily cross borders, there is a need for international cooperation and harmonization of laws to ensure consistent treatment and protection across jurisdictions. Organizations like the World Intellectual Property Organization (WIPO) are beginning to explore these issues, but significant work remains to be done to create a coherent global framework.

Moving Towards a Comprehensive Regulatory Approach

As AI technologies continue to evolve and their creative capabilities expand, the need for specific regulations to address the IP status of AI-generated works will become increasingly urgent. Policymakers, legal scholars, and industry stakeholders must work together to develop a regulatory framework that balances the need for innovation and creativity with the protection of rights and the prevention of abuses. This may involve a combination of revising existing laws, creating new legal categories, and establishing clear guidelines for ownership, authorship, and liability in the context of AI-generated works.

Analysis of Existing Laws: Copyright Act, Patent Act, Lanham Act, and Defend Trade Secrets Act (DTSA)

The existing intellectual property (IP) laws in the United States were primarily designed to protect the creative works, inventions, trademarks, and confidential information of human creators. As a result, these laws present unique challenges when applied to AI-generated works, given their reliance on human authorship, inventorship, and creativity. This section provides an in-depth analysis of how the major U.S. IP laws — the Copyright Act, Patent Act, Lanham Act, and Defend Trade Secrets Act (DTSA) — currently address, or fail to address, the complexities introduced by AI-generated works.

Copyright Act of 1976

The Copyright Act of 1976 governs the protection of "original works of authorship" that are fixed in a tangible medium of expression. This law covers a wide range of creative works, including literary works, music, visual art, and software, among others. However, the Copyright Act assumes that the "author" is a human being.

- **Requirement of Human Authorship:** Under the Copyright Act, a work must be created by a human author to qualify for copyright protection. The U.S. Copyright Office's Compendium of U.S. Copyright Office Practices clarifies that works produced by machines, devices, or processes operating randomly or automatically without any creative input or intervention from a human do not qualify for registration. This position effectively excludes works generated autonomously by AI from copyright protection, as demonstrated by cases like *Thaler v. Copyright Office*, where an AI-created image was denied copyright registration due to the lack of human authorship.

- **Originality and Creativity Standards:** Copyright law also requires that a work display a minimum level of originality, which is generally interpreted as human creativity. AI-generated works, particularly those created autonomously, may struggle to meet this requirement because they lack the human element traditionally associated with creativity. The law does not currently recognize AI as capable of original thought or expression, leading to significant gaps in protection for these works.

- **Potential Revisions Needed:** To address these gaps, potential revisions to the Copyright Act could include expanding the definition of "authorship" to include AI-generated works or creating a new category for machine-generated content. However, such changes would require careful consideration of how to balance the protection of human creativity with the encouragement of technological innovation.

Patent Act

The Patent Act governs the protection of inventions, granting exclusive rights to inventors for new, useful, and non-obvious inventions. The Act is designed to incentivize innovation by granting inventors a temporary monopoly on the use and commercialization of their inventions.

- **Human Inventorship Requirement:** Under the current Patent Act, only "natural persons" can be recognized as inventors. This requirement has been reinforced by the U.S. Patent and

Trademark Office (USPTO) and by courts, which have consistently ruled that AI cannot be considered an inventor. For example, in 2020, the USPTO rejected patent applications listing an AI as the inventor, emphasizing that the law requires inventors to be human. As a result, any invention generated autonomously by AI cannot currently receive patent protection, raising concerns about how to protect valuable technological advancements made by machines.

- **Challenges for AI-Generated Inventions:** AI is increasingly capable of creating innovative solutions to complex problems, often producing inventions that are novel, useful, and non-obvious. However, the current legal framework does not provide a clear path for protecting these inventions, potentially disincentivizing companies from investing in AI research and development.

- **Possible Legal Adjustments:** To accommodate AI-generated inventions, potential adjustments to the Patent Act could include allowing for joint inventorship between humans and AI or recognizing AI systems as co-inventors under specific conditions. Alternatively, a new legal framework could be developed to address the unique characteristics of AI-generated inventions.

Lanham Act

The Lanham Act governs trademarks, service marks, and unfair competition in the United States. It is primarily concerned with protecting consumers from confusion and deception by ensuring that trademarks are distinctive and indicate the source of goods or services.

- **Trademarks and AI:** Trademarks can theoretically be generated by AI, especially when AI is used to create new logos, brand names, or slogans. However, the Lanham Act does not explicitly address the use of AI in generating trademarks or the ownership of AI-generated marks. This lack of clarity presents challenges in determining who owns the rights to a trademark created by AI — the person or entity who owns the AI, the developer of the AI, or the user who commissioned the AI-generated mark.

- **Issues of Distinctiveness and Use in Commerce:** For a trademark to be eligible for protection under the Lanham Act, it must be distinctive and used in commerce. Determining whether an AI-generated mark meets these criteria involves complex legal questions, such as whether the AI or its owner can establish the required intent to use the mark in commerce and whether the mark is sufficiently distinctive.
- **Potential Areas for Reform:** To address the growing use of AI in branding and marketing, amendments to the Lanham Act could clarify the treatment of AI-generated trademarks, including ownership rights, registration requirements, and enforcement mechanisms.

Defend Trade Secrets Act (DTSA)

The Defend Trade Secrets Act (DTSA) provides federal protection for trade secrets, defined as information that derives independent economic value from not being generally known and that is subject to reasonable efforts to maintain its secrecy. Trade secrets can include formulas, practices, designs, processes, or any confidential business information.

- **Relevance to AI-Generated Works:** AI can both create and protect trade secrets. For example, an AI algorithm that autonomously generates new product designs or manufacturing processes could produce trade secrets. Similarly, AI can be used to protect trade secrets by analyzing data to detect leaks or unauthorized access.
- **Ownership and Protection Issues:** The DTSA protects the owner of a trade secret from misappropriation, but it does not specifically address whether trade secrets created by AI are eligible for protection or who owns such secrets. If an AI generates a valuable business process or formula without human input, it remains unclear whether the developer of the AI, the user, or another party holds the rights to the trade secret.
- **Implications for AI-Generated Trade Secrets:** To address the complexities introduced by AI, amendments to the DTSA could provide guidance on the ownership and protection of trade secrets generated by AI. This could include defining who is considered

the "owner" of a trade secret created by AI and under what conditions AI-generated information qualifies as a trade secret.

Overall Legal Implications and Need for Reform

The analysis of these existing laws reveals that the current U.S. intellectual property framework is not well-equipped to handle the unique challenges posed by AI-generated works. The requirement for human authorship, inventorship, and use in commerce creates significant gaps in protection, leaving many AI-generated works without adequate legal recognition or safeguards.

- **Need for New Legal Categories or Adjustments:** To address these gaps, new legal categories or frameworks may be necessary. This could involve redefining key concepts like authorship and inventorship, developing specific provisions for AI-generated works, or creating entirely new categories of protection tailored to the unique characteristics of AI.
- **Harmonization and International Considerations:** Given the global nature of AI technology and IP, there is also a need for harmonization of laws across jurisdictions to provide consistent treatment of AI-generated works. International organizations, such as WIPO, may play a key role in developing guidelines and standards to address these issues.

Relevant Legal Precedents: Thaler v. Copyright Office Case, Patent Applications for AI Systems, etc.

Recent legal precedents in the United States highlight the challenges of applying existing intellectual property laws to AI-generated works. These cases illustrate the limitations of current frameworks and provide insight into how courts and regulatory bodies interpret the law concerning machine-generated content. This section examines key cases such as *Thaler v. Copyright Office* and patent applications for AI systems to understand how the legal system is responding to these emerging issues.

Thaler v. Copyright Office

The *Thaler v. Copyright Office* case is a landmark legal battle that addresses the question of whether AI-generated works can be copyrighted under U.S. law. The case was initiated by Stephen Thaler, an AI developer who sought copyright protection for an image created autonomously by his AI system, known as the Creativity Machine.

- **Background of the Case:** Thaler's AI, the Creativity Machine, generated an image titled "A Recent Entrance to Paradise." Thaler applied to the U.S. Copyright Office for copyright registration of the image, listing the AI as the author and himself as the owner of the copyright. The application was rejected by the Copyright Office on the grounds that the image lacked human authorship, which is a requirement for copyright protection under U.S. law.

- **Court's Decision and Rationale:** In 2022, the U.S. District Court for the District of Columbia upheld the Copyright Office's decision, affirming that copyright law requires a human author. The court ruled that works created by non-human entities, including AI, are not eligible for copyright protection under the Copyright Act of 1976. The decision emphasized that the Copyright Act and historical legal interpretations require "some element of human creativity" to qualify for protection.

- **Implications of the Case:** The *Thaler v. Copyright Office* case set a critical precedent, reinforcing the principle that only works created by humans can be copyrighted in the United States. This ruling has significant implications for creators, developers, and businesses using AI to generate content, as it effectively excludes fully autonomous AI-generated works from copyright protection. The case also raises broader questions about the future of copyright law and whether legislative changes are needed to address the realities of AI-generated content.

Patent Applications for AI Systems: DABUS and the AI Inventor Debate

Another significant area of legal precedent involves patent applications for inventions created by AI systems. The most notable example is the case involving DABUS (Device for the Autonomous Bootstrapping of Unified Sentience), an AI system developed by Stephen Thaler, which has been at the center of a global debate on whether AI can be recognized as an inventor.

- **Background of the DABUS Case:** In 2019, Thaler filed patent applications in multiple countries, including the United States, listing DABUS as the inventor of two inventions: a fractal beverage container and a neural flame device for attracting attention in emergencies. The applications sought to establish that an AI system, DABUS, could be considered the inventor, arguing that the inventions were generated autonomously by the AI without any direct human involvement in the creative process.

- **USPTO Decision and Court Rulings:** The U.S. Patent and Trademark Office (USPTO) rejected the patent applications, stating that U.S. patent law requires inventors to be natural persons. The USPTO's decision was upheld by the U.S. District Court for the Eastern District of Virginia in 2021, which ruled that the Patent Act, as currently written, does not permit non-human entities to be recognized as inventors. The court emphasized that the term "individual" in the Patent Act refers to human beings, and therefore, only humans can be named as inventors on a patent application.

- **Global Context and Divergent Approaches:** The DABUS case has sparked a global discussion about the status of AI-generated inventions. While the U.S., UK, and European Patent Offices have all rejected the notion of AI as an inventor, other jurisdictions, such as South Africa and Australia, have taken a different approach, allowing patents to be granted with AI listed as an inventor. These divergent approaches highlight the lack of international consensus on this issue and the potential for further legal and policy developments.

- **Implications of the Case:** The rulings in the DABUS case underscore the challenges of applying existing patent laws to AI-generated inventions. They also illustrate the need for potential reforms to address the unique characteristics of AI-generated innovations, such as the possibility of recognizing AI as a co-inventor or establishing new categories of protection for inventions developed by AI.

Additional Relevant Cases and Regulatory Actions

Several other legal cases and regulatory actions provide further context on how U.S. intellectual property law is dealing with AI-generated works:

- **Feist Publications, Inc. v. Rural Telephone Service Co., Inc. (1991):** Although not directly related to AI, this Supreme Court case established the principle that copyright requires a minimal degree of creativity, a standard that has implications for AI-generated works. The ruling clarifies that mere mechanical reproduction or creation does not meet the threshold for copyright protection, reinforcing the human creativity requirement.
- **United States v. Athalye (2015):** This case involved the theft of trade secrets but indirectly touched upon the role of AI and machine learning in analyzing and protecting trade secrets. It illustrates the complexities of applying existing trade secret laws to cases where AI systems are involved in the creation, storage, or protection of confidential information.
- **USPTO Requests for Public Comment (2019 and 2020):** The USPTO has taken steps to engage with the public and industry stakeholders on the issues surrounding AI and IP. In 2019 and 2020, the USPTO issued requests for public comment on the use of AI in IP, including questions on the inventorship of AI-generated inventions and the authorship of AI-generated works. These efforts indicate a recognition by the USPTO of the need to adapt IP laws to accommodate technological advancements, though no definitive changes have yet been made.

Key Takeaways from Legal Precedents

The legal precedents discussed above highlight several key points regarding the current U.S. IP framework and its approach to AI-generated works:

- **Reaffirmation of Human-Centric IP Laws:** U.S. courts and regulatory bodies have consistently reaffirmed that existing IP laws are centered around human authorship, inventorship, and creativity. This poses significant challenges for AI-generated works that do not involve direct human involvement.

- **Need for Legislative and Policy Reforms:** The legal decisions suggest a growing awareness of the limitations of current laws and the potential need for legislative or policy reforms to address the unique characteristics of AI-generated works. Possible reforms could include redefining authorship and inventorship, creating new categories of protection, or establishing guidelines for liability and enforcement.

- **Divergent Global Approaches:** The contrasting decisions on AI inventorship in different jurisdictions underscore the lack of international consensus on this issue. This divergence may prompt further debate and cooperation among countries to harmonize their IP laws in light of AI advancements.

Future Directions for Legal Precedents in AI-Generated IP

As AI technologies continue to advance and become more integrated into creative and inventive processes, further legal challenges and cases are likely to emerge. Future directions could include:

- **Development of New Legal Doctrines:** Courts may develop new legal doctrines or interpretations to accommodate the complexities of AI-generated works, potentially recognizing new forms of authorship or inventorship.

- **Increased Involvement of International Organizations:** International bodies such as the World Intellectual Property Organization (WIPO) may play a more prominent role in developing global standards and frameworks to address the IP challenges posed by AI.

- **Continued Evolution of Case Law:** As more disputes involving AI-generated works are litigated, U.S. case law will continue to evolve, providing greater clarity on the application of existing laws and highlighting areas where further reform is needed.

Determining Ownership:

Who Is the Author? Perspectives from Human Authors, Machine Owners, and Algorithm Developers

Determining the ownership of AI-generated works presents one of the most significant and controversial challenges in intellectual property law. Traditional IP laws in the United States are built around the premise of human authorship, where a human creator is easily identifiable. However, when a work is generated by an AI system, identifying the "author" and rightful owner of the IP rights becomes complex. This section examines the various perspectives on authorship and ownership, including those of human authors, machine owners, and algorithm developers, and explores the implications of each viewpoint.

Human Authors: The Role of Creative Input and Control

One perspective suggests that human authors should retain ownership rights to AI-generated works if they have contributed significant creative input or maintained control over the creation process.

- **Creative Input and Human Control:** Proponents of this view argue that when a human uses AI as a tool or assistant to create a work, the human's creative direction and decision-making should qualify them as the author. For example, an artist who uses AI software to generate digital art or a writer who uses AI to suggest plotlines or dialogue still exercises creative control over the final product. In such cases, the human is seen as the primary creative force, with the AI serving merely as a tool that facilitates the process.

- **Legal Precedents Supporting Human Authorship:** Current U.S. copyright law aligns with this perspective. The U.S. Copyright Office has consistently stated that works must have a ·human author to be eligible for copyright protection. If a human is involved in the creative process, even if an AI is used as a tool, the human can be considered the author and hold the copyright. This interpretation upholds the traditional standards of originality and creativity, which are central to IP law.

- **Challenges with This Perspective:** The challenge arises when AI plays a more significant role in the creation process. If the AI is responsible for generating substantial portions of the work, the line between the human's creative contribution and the machine's output becomes blurred. Determining the threshold of human input required to claim authorship becomes a contentious issue. For example, if an AI system autonomously generates a piece of music based on parameters set by a human, who is the true author?

Machine Owners: Ownership Based on Possession and Investment

Another perspective argues that the owner of the machine (the AI system) that generated the work should be recognized as the rightful owner of the IP rights. This viewpoint is based on the notion that ownership should be linked to possession and the investment made in developing or acquiring the AI.

- **Rationale for Ownership by Machine Owners:** Advocates of this view argue that the owner of the AI system is best positioned to claim ownership because they have invested in the creation, maintenance, and operation of the machine. This investment includes the costs of hardware, software, training datasets, and other resources necessary to develop and run the AI. From this perspective, the machine owner bears the risks and costs associated with the AI's operation and should therefore benefit from any commercial exploitation of the AI-generated work.
- **Analogies to Ownership of Tools and Equipment:** This perspective draws analogies to traditional ownership principles where the owner of a tool or piece of equipment typically owns the products or outputs created by that tool. For example, a company that owns a 3D printer would own the objects produced by the printer, even if the printer is highly automated. Similarly, the owner of an AI system could be considered the owner of the works it generates.
- **Legal Challenges and Limitations:** The current U.S. IP framework does not directly support this perspective because it is heavily focused on human authorship and creativity.

Moreover, defining "ownership" based solely on investment or possession could lead to ethical and practical issues, such as monopolistic control over creative outputs by entities that own large-scale AI systems. This could stifle competition and innovation, particularly if a few companies control the majority of AI-generated works.

Algorithm Developers: Ownership Rights Based on Software Creation

A third perspective suggests that the developers of the AI algorithms that generate the works should be considered the rightful owners of the IP rights. This argument is rooted in the notion that the developers are the ones who create the underlying code and algorithms that enable the AI to function creatively.

- **Justification for Developer Ownership:** Proponents argue that since the developers design and program the AI's core capabilities, they should be entitled to ownership of the works generated by that AI. In this view, the creativity involved in developing the algorithms and training the AI model equates to the creativity required to produce traditional works of authorship. Thus, the developer's contribution is seen as fundamental to the creation of any AI-generated output.
- **Implications for Open Source and Proprietary Software Models:** The question of developer ownership becomes particularly complex in cases involving open-source software or collaborative development environments. If the AI is built using open-source code contributed by multiple developers, determining who holds the ownership rights to AI-generated works becomes challenging. Conversely, if the AI is developed using proprietary software owned by a single entity, that entity could claim ownership of all works generated by the AI, potentially leading to concerns about market concentration and reduced access to creative tools.
- **Limitations Under Current Law:** Under current U.S. IP law, the idea of developer ownership is not explicitly recognized. Intellectual property rights typically pertain to the end product

rather than the tools or methods used to create it. Furthermore, granting ownership to developers could conflict with the rights of users or machine owners who deploy the AI in various creative contexts. There is also the challenge of defining the scope of the developer's ownership: does it extend to every work generated by the AI in all contexts, or only in specific cases?

Hybrid Approaches and Shared Ownership Models

Given the complexities of assigning ownership to a single party, some experts propose hybrid or shared ownership models that account for the multiple contributors involved in creating AI-generated works.

- **Joint Ownership Models:** One proposed solution is a joint ownership model where multiple parties, such as the human operator, machine owner, and algorithm developer, share ownership of the AI-generated work. This approach could ensure that all stakeholders with a significant role in the creation process are recognized and compensated. However, joint ownership models also present challenges in terms of managing rights, enforcing IP protections, and dividing royalties or profits.

- **Licensing and Contractual Agreements:** Another approach involves using licensing and contractual agreements to clarify ownership and usage rights for AI-generated works. For example, developers and machine owners could enter into agreements that specify the terms of ownership and compensation for any works generated by the AI. These agreements could help mitigate legal uncertainties and disputes, but they may also require significant negotiation and legal oversight.

- **Public Domain or Non-Exclusive Rights:** Some commentators suggest that fully autonomous AI-generated works should be considered public domain, as they lack human authorship and therefore do not qualify for traditional IP protections. Alternatively, non-exclusive rights could be granted to multiple parties, allowing for broader use and dissemination while still recognizing the contributions of various stakeholders.

Future Directions and Considerations for Determining Ownership

The debate over who should own AI-generated works reflects broader questions about the purpose of intellectual property law and the role of human creativity in the digital age. Future directions for addressing ownership issues may include:

- **Reforming IP Laws:** Legislative reforms may be necessary to adapt existing IP laws to the realities of AI-generated works. This could involve redefining authorship to include AI-generated content, establishing new categories of protection, or creating guidelines for shared or hybrid ownership models.
- **Developing International Norms:** Given the global nature of AI technologies and creative industries, there is a need for international cooperation to develop harmonized norms and standards for determining ownership of AI-generated works.
- **Encouraging Ethical Practices:** Beyond legal reforms, there is also a need to encourage ethical practices among developers, machine owners, and users of AI. This includes promoting transparency, fairness, and accountability in the creation and commercialization of AI-generated content.

Issues of Originality and "Human Creativity" Requirements in Copyright

One of the core principles of copyright law is the requirement of originality and human creativity. For a work to qualify for copyright protection under U.S. law, it must be both original and the product of human authorship. This presents significant challenges for AI-generated works, which may not meet these criteria as traditionally defined. This section explores the concept of originality, the human creativity requirement in copyright law, and how these concepts impact the copyright eligibility of AI-generated works.

Understanding the Requirement of Originality in Copyright Law

The requirement of originality is fundamental to copyright protection in the United States. The U.S. Supreme Court, in *Feist Publications, Inc. v. Rural Telephone Service Co.* (1991), clarified that to be original, a work must possess at least a minimal degree of creativity. This means that the

174

work must be independently created by the author (not copied from another work) and demonstrate some level of creative expression.

- **Minimal Creativity Standard:** The "minimal creativity" standard set forth in *Feist* requires that a work demonstrate a modicum of creativity. This does not mean that the work must be novel or highly artistic, but it must reflect some original expression by a human author. Simple compilations of facts, for instance, do not qualify for copyright protection unless they involve creative selection, arrangement, or coordination.

- **Implications for AI-Generated Works:** AI-generated works challenge this standard because they may lack the "human" element traditionally required for originality. An AI system, particularly when operating autonomously, does not possess human consciousness, intent, or creative thought. While an AI can produce content that appears creative, the absence of human authorship complicates its eligibility for copyright protection under the current legal framework.

The Human Creativity Requirement: Legal Interpretations and Limitations

Copyright law presupposes that creativity originates from human intellect and imagination. This human-centric approach is embedded in both statutory law and judicial interpretations, and it reflects the philosophical foundations of copyright as a means to encourage human artistic and literary expression.

- **Human-Centric Focus of Copyright Law:** The Copyright Act of 1976 and subsequent legal interpretations have consistently emphasized that copyright protection is intended for works created by human authors. The U.S. Copyright Office's Compendium of U.S. Copyright Office Practices explicitly states that works produced by machines or processes that operate autonomously or randomly, without human input or intervention, are not eligible for copyright registration.

- **Judicial Precedents Reinforcing Human Creativity:** In cases like *Thaler v. Copyright Office*, courts have reiterated that copyright protection is unavailable for works lacking human authorship. The decision emphasized that copyright law is intended to protect human intellectual output, not the outputs of machines. This interpretation aligns with the general principle that copyright incentivizes human creativity by granting exclusive rights to authors for their original works.

- **Limitations in Applying Human Creativity to AI Works:** While this human-centric focus provides clarity for traditional works, it presents limitations for AI-generated content. AI systems, particularly those using advanced machine learning techniques, can produce works that are highly original in appearance but lack the human intent or creative spark traditionally required. The inability of current law to recognize the originality of AI-generated works leaves a significant gap in protection, which could deter investment and innovation in AI technologies.

Challenges of Defining Originality for AI-Generated Works

Determining whether AI-generated works meet the originality and creativity requirements under copyright law presents several challenges:

- **Lack of Human Intent or Creative Input:** AI-generated works often lack human intent or creative input, particularly when created autonomously. For example, if an AI system generates a poem or a painting without any human guidance or intervention, it is difficult to argue that the work reflects human creativity. The absence of a human "author" who consciously creates or expresses an idea is a key barrier to establishing originality.
- **Role of Training Data and Algorithms:** AI systems learn from vast datasets, which may include copyrighted works. As a result, there are concerns that AI-generated works may not be truly "original" if they heavily draw from or resemble the works included in their training data. This raises questions about whether AI-generated works are sufficiently independent to be considered original or whether they are derivative works that lack the necessary creativity.

- **Unpredictability and Complexity of AI Outputs:** AI-generated works can be highly complex and unpredictable, often exceeding the understanding or intent of the human developers who created the algorithms. This complexity makes it difficult to trace the source of creativity in such works, complicating the assessment of originality. If the AI system generates output that is so advanced or unexpected that it cannot be attributed to any specific human input, courts and regulators face a challenge in determining whether the work should be eligible for copyright protection.

Potential Approaches to Addressing the Originality Requirement for AI-Generated Works

Given these challenges, various legal scholars and policymakers have proposed potential approaches to address the originality requirement for AI-generated works:

- **Expanding the Definition of Authorship:** One approach is to expand the definition of "authorship" to include AI-generated works. This could involve recognizing the human developers, users, or owners of the AI as the authors, even when the work is generated autonomously by the machine. This approach would require legislative changes to the Copyright Act to redefine authorship in a way that encompasses AI-generated content.
- **Creating a New Category for AI-Generated Works:** Another proposal is to create a new category of IP protection specifically for AI-generated works. This category could have its own rules for originality, authorship, and protection duration. For example, works generated autonomously by AI could receive a shorter duration of protection or be subject to different rules regarding licensing and use.
- **Relying on Alternative IP Protections:** In cases where AI-generated works do not meet the requirements for copyright, other forms of IP protection, such as trade secrets or trademarks, may be more appropriate. For example, an AI-generated logo might qualify for trademark protection if it is used in commerce and serves as a source identifier. Similarly, the underlying data

or algorithms used to create AI-generated works could be protected as trade secrets if they meet the criteria for confidentiality and competitive value.

The Broader Implications of Maintaining the Human Creativity Requirement

Maintaining the current human creativity requirement has broader implications for the future of copyright law and the development of AI technologies:

- **Balancing Human Creativity and Technological Innovation:** While the human creativity requirement preserves the traditional focus of copyright law, it may also create barriers to innovation. By excluding AI-generated works from copyright protection, the law could discourage investment in AI research and development, particularly in the creative industries.
- **Addressing Ethical and Policy Concerns:** Expanding copyright protection to include AI-generated works raises ethical and policy concerns, such as the potential for monopolization of creative outputs by entities that control large-scale AI systems. Ensuring that the expansion of copyright to AI works does not undermine public access to knowledge and culture will be a critical challenge for policymakers.
- **Encouraging International Harmonization:** Given the global nature of AI technologies and content creation, there is a need for international harmonization of copyright laws to address AI-generated works consistently. International organizations, such as the World Intellectual Property Organization (WIPO), may play a crucial role in developing guidelines and standards that balance the protection of human creativity with the realities of AI-generated content.

Moving Forward: Reevaluating the Role of Originality in Copyright

As AI continues to evolve and play an increasingly significant role in creative processes, it may be necessary to reevaluate the role of originality and human creativity in copyright law. This could involve exploring new legal frameworks, redefining key concepts, or developing alternative protections to ensure that both human and AI-generated works are adequately protected and incentivized.

Liability Concerns in Case of Rights Violations

Liability Concerns in Case of Rights Violations Biased Algorithms, Operational Errors, and Misappropriation of Human Rights

Liability concerns represent a significant challenge in the context of AI-generated works, especially when rights violations occur due to biased algorithms, operational errors, or the misappropriation of human rights. Determining who is legally responsible when AI systems produce harmful or infringing content is a complex issue that current legal frameworks are not fully equipped to handle. This section explores the different types of liability concerns related to AI-generated works and the potential legal implications for developers, owners, users, and other stakeholders.

Liability for Biased Algorithms and Discriminatory Outputs

AI systems can inadvertently produce biased or discriminatory content due to the data on which they are trained or the algorithms that govern their behavior. When biased AI-generated works infringe upon individuals' rights or result in discrimination, questions arise about who is liable for the harm caused.

- **Sources of Algorithmic Bias:** Algorithmic bias occurs when AI systems reflect or amplify biases present in their training data or the algorithms themselves. For example, an AI trained on biased data might generate content that reflects racial, gender, or cultural prejudices. This can lead to discriminatory outcomes in various domains, including hiring processes, credit scoring, and creative content generation (e.g., stereotyped representations in images or text).
- **Potential Defendants in Bias-Related Cases:** When AI-generated works result in biased or discriminatory content, several parties could potentially be held liable:
    - **Developers and Programmers:** The creators of the AI algorithms may be held responsible if the bias is traced back

to flaws or biases in the code or the choice of training data. Developers might face liability for negligence in designing or testing the AI system.

- o **Data Providers:** Entities that supply the training data could be liable if the data is inherently biased or insufficiently representative, leading to biased AI outputs.
- o **Users and Operators:** Individuals or organizations that deploy biased AI systems could also be held accountable, especially if they fail to monitor and mitigate bias in the AI's outputs.

- • **Legal Frameworks and Standards:** Currently, U.S. law does not provide clear guidelines for liability in cases of algorithmic bias. However, anti-discrimination laws, such as the Civil Rights Act, may apply if biased AI-generated outputs lead to unlawful discrimination. Additionally, regulatory bodies, like the Federal Trade Commission (FTC), may intervene if biased outputs constitute unfair or deceptive practices.

Liability for Operational Errors and Defective AI Systems

AI systems are prone to operational errors, which can lead to rights violations or other harmful outcomes. When an AI system malfunctions or produces unintended outputs, determining liability becomes critical to resolving disputes and compensating affected parties.

- • **Types of Operational Errors:** Operational errors in AI systems can include:

- o **Programming Errors:** Mistakes in the code that cause the AI to behave unpredictably or produce unintended results.
- o **System Failures:** Hardware or software failures that result in loss of data or incorrect outputs.
- o **Human-AI Interaction Errors:** Miscommunications or misunderstandings between human operators and the AI system, leading to erroneous outputs.

- • **Liability Frameworks for Defective AI Systems:** Liability for operational errors in AI-generated works could be governed by several legal doctrines:

- o **Product Liability Law:** If an AI system is considered a "product," developers or manufacturers could be liable under product liability laws for defects that cause harm. This approach would treat AI developers similarly to traditional manufacturers who are responsible for ensuring their products are safe and reliable.
- o **Negligence and Duty of Care:** Developers, operators, and users of AI systems could be held liable under negligence principles if they fail to exercise reasonable care in developing, deploying, or managing AI systems, and that failure results in harm. Courts would need to assess whether the parties involved acted with due diligence and took appropriate steps to prevent foreseeable errors.
- o **Contractual Liability:** In cases where AI systems are provided under contract, liability for operational errors may be determined by the terms of the contract. Contracts could include clauses that limit or specify liability in cases of malfunction, error, or damage caused by AI-generated outputs.

- **Challenges in Applying Traditional Liability Doctrines:** Applying traditional liability doctrines to AI-generated works is not straightforward. Unlike traditional products, AI systems are dynamic and continuously learning, which complicates the identification of a single point of failure or defect. Additionally, the involvement of multiple parties (developers, data providers, users) in the AI ecosystem makes it challenging to assign responsibility clearly.

Liability for Misappropriation of Human Rights

AI-generated works can potentially misappropriate or infringe upon human rights, such as privacy, intellectual property, and freedom of expression. When AI outputs violate these rights, determining liability can be complex, particularly if the violation was unintentional or unforeseen.

- **Examples of Human Rights Violations by AI:**
  - ○ **Privacy Violations:** AI systems that analyze or generate content based on personal data can infringe on privacy rights, particularly if the data is used without consent or in ways that violate data protection laws, such as the General Data Protection Regulation (GDPR) in the European Union.
  - ○ **Intellectual Property Infringement:** AI-generated works that are substantially similar to copyrighted material could infringe on the intellectual property rights of the original creators. For example, if an AI generates a new piece of music that closely resembles an existing copyrighted song, there could be grounds for a copyright infringement claim.
  - ○ **Defamation and Misinformation:** AI systems that generate false or misleading information, such as deepfakes or fake news, can harm individuals' reputations and violate their right to be free from defamation or slander.

- **Liability Frameworks for Human Rights Violations by AI:**
  - ○ **Direct Liability for Developers and Operators:** In cases where AI systems violate human rights, developers and operators may face direct liability, especially if they failed to implement adequate safeguards to prevent such violations. Courts may consider factors such as the foreseeability of the harm, the degree of control the developers or operators had over the AI, and whether reasonable measures were taken to mitigate risks.
  - ○ **Vicarious Liability for Employers:** If AI-generated works violate human rights in the course of employment or business activities, employers could be held vicariously liable for the actions of their employees or agents who deployed or managed the AI systems.
  - ○ **Regulatory Enforcement and Penalties:** Regulatory bodies, such as the FTC in the U.S., may enforce penalties against companies that deploy AI systems resulting in rights violations, particularly if the companies engaged in unfair or

deceptive practices. Additionally, data protection authorities may impose fines for violations of privacy laws.

- **Challenges in Addressing Human Rights Violations by AI:** The dynamic and autonomous nature of AI systems makes it difficult to anticipate all potential rights violations. Determining liability requires establishing a clear causal link between the AI system's outputs and the harm caused, which can be challenging when multiple parties are involved or when the AI operates independently.

Mitigating Liability Risks: Best Practices and Policy Recommendations

To mitigate liability risks associated with AI-generated works, stakeholders should consider adopting best practices and implementing robust policies:

- **Algorithmic Audits and Bias Mitigation:** Regularly auditing AI algorithms for bias and ensuring diverse and representative training data can help reduce the risk of biased outputs. Developers should implement fairness and transparency standards and document their decision-making processes to demonstrate compliance with ethical guidelines.
- **Clear Documentation and Accountability Measures:** Developers, users, and operators should maintain clear documentation of AI systems' design, development, and deployment processes. Establishing accountability measures and assigning roles and responsibilities can help clarify liability in the event of errors or rights violations.
- **Adopting Safe AI Development Practices:** Implementing safety measures, such as testing AI systems under various conditions, creating fail-safes, and conducting impact assessments, can help prevent operational errors and mitigate potential harms.
- **Using Contractual Agreements to Define Liability:** Stakeholders can use contractual agreements to specify liability terms, including limitations of liability, indemnity clauses, and

warranties. Such agreements can provide clarity and reduce disputes when AI-generated works result in harm.

The Need for Legal Reform and Clarification

Given the complexities and challenges in assigning liability for AI-generated works, there is a growing need for legal reform and clarification:

- **Developing Specific AI Liability Laws:** Legislators may need to create specific laws that address liability issues unique to AI, such as joint liability frameworks for multi-party collaborations, product liability standards for AI systems, and rules for algorithmic accountability.

- **Encouraging International Cooperation:** Since AI-generated works and their impacts are not confined by borders, there is a need for international cooperation to harmonize liability standards and develop consistent guidelines for addressing AI-related rights violations.

- **Promoting Ethical AI Development:** Governments and regulatory bodies should promote ethical AI development through guidelines, standards, and incentives, ensuring that developers prioritize safety, fairness, and transparency in their AI systems.

By addressing these liability concerns, policymakers, developers, and stakeholders can work together to ensure that AI-generated works are created and used in a way that respects rights, minimizes risks, and fosters innovation.

Chapter 9:
Legal Tools and Protection Models for AI-Generated Works

Applying Copyright: Extending the Concept of "Authorship" to Machines

As AI-generated works become increasingly prevalent, there is a growing debate about how copyright law should apply to these creations. One of the most significant challenges is the question of whether the concept of "authorship" can, or should, be extended to include AI-generated works. Current copyright laws in the United States and many other jurisdictions are based on the presumption that only human beings can be authors. However, some legal scholars and policymakers are exploring the possibility of adapting copyright laws to recognize AI-generated works, either by extending the definition of authorship or creating new legal categories for these creations. This section examines the potential legal and practical implications of extending the concept of authorship to machines.

The Current Definition of Authorship and Its Limitations

Under the U.S. Copyright Act of 1976, "authorship" is a fundamental requirement for copyright protection. A work must be an original expression of authorship fixed in a tangible medium to qualify for copyright. The law, as it stands, assumes that the author must be a human being. The U.S. Copyright Office's Compendium of U.S. Copyright Office Practices explicitly states that works created by a machine or automated process without human intervention are not eligible for copyright registration.

- **Human-Centric Definition of Authorship:** The human-centric focus of the current copyright framework is grounded in the belief that only humans can possess the intellectual and creative capabilities needed to produce original works. This approach reflects a longstanding legal and philosophical tradition that links creativity to human consciousness, intention, and moral rights.

- **Limitations of the Current Framework:** The traditional definition of authorship creates significant limitations when applied to AI-generated works. These works can range from literary content, visual art, and music to more complex creations like software code or architectural designs, all produced autonomously by AI systems. If AI-generated works are excluded from copyright protection due to the lack of human authorship, this could undermine the incentive structure for the development and commercialization of AI technologies and diminish the economic value of these creations.

Potential Approaches to Extending the Concept of Authorship

To address these limitations, several approaches have been proposed to extend or adapt the concept of authorship to include AI-generated works:

- **Recognizing AI as a "Legal Author":** One approach is to recognize AI systems as "legal authors" for the purposes of copyright law. This would involve granting the AI itself certain legal rights and responsibilities, much like corporate entities can hold copyrights and enter into contracts. This concept is highly controversial, as it challenges fundamental principles of personhood and agency in the law. It would require a significant rethinking of legal doctrines and might raise concerns about accountability, as AI lacks consciousness, intention, and moral agency.

- **Attributing Authorship to the AI's Human Developers or Operators:** Another approach is to attribute authorship to the human developers or operators of the AI system. This could involve recognizing the individual or entity that programmed or owns the AI as the author, based on their role in creating the underlying technology or setting the parameters for the AI's output. This method aligns more closely with existing legal principles, as it keeps the concept of authorship grounded in human activity. However, it could also lead to disputes over

186

ownership when multiple parties are involved in developing, training, or operating the AI.

- **Creating a New Category of "Machine-Assisted" Works:** A less radical approach is to create a new legal category for "machine-assisted" works, where copyright could be granted based on a combination of human and machine input. For example, if a human provides substantial guidance, supervision, or creative input in the use of an AI tool, they could be recognized as the author, with the AI's role acknowledged as an assisting tool. This approach would require a new legal framework to determine the extent of human involvement needed to qualify for copyright and to clarify how rights are shared or transferred.

Implications of Extending Authorship to Machines

Extending the concept of authorship to machines would have wide-ranging legal, economic, and ethical implications:

- **Legal Implications:**
  - **Redefining Copyright Law:** Extending authorship to machines would require significant changes to existing copyright laws. It would involve redefining core concepts like originality, creativity, and intent to accommodate non-human authors. This could lead to challenges in enforcement and interpretation, as courts would need to develop new criteria to evaluate AI-generated works.
  - **Impact on Moral Rights:** In jurisdictions that recognize moral rights (such as the right to attribution or the right to object to derogatory treatment of a work), extending authorship to machines could complicate the application of these rights. AI systems lack human dignity and moral considerations, raising questions about how, or whether, moral rights would apply to machine-generated works.

- **Economic Implications:**
  - **Incentivizing AI Development:** Extending copyright protection to AI-generated works could incentivize further investment in AI technologies, as developers and companies

would have legal protections for the outputs generated by their systems. This could encourage innovation and growth in industries that rely on AI, such as content creation, entertainment, design, and software development.

- o **Potential Monopolization Concerns:** On the other hand, extending authorship to machines could lead to monopolization of creative outputs by entities that control large-scale AI systems. If a few companies own the rights to vast quantities of AI-generated works, this could stifle competition and limit access to creative content and tools for smaller players.

- **Ethical Implications:**

  - o **Fairness and Equity:** There are ethical concerns about fairness and equity in recognizing machines as authors. Some argue that extending copyright to AI-generated works would diminish the value of human creativity and undermine the social and cultural significance of human-created works. Others worry about exacerbating inequalities if copyright protection disproportionately benefits corporations that can afford to develop or acquire advanced AI systems.

  - o **Accountability and Responsibility:** If machines are granted legal authorship, questions arise about accountability and responsibility. For example, if an AI system generates infringing or harmful content, who would be held responsible? Recognizing machines as authors without clear guidelines for accountability could create legal loopholes and complicate enforcement.

Legal Precedents and Policy Proposals

Several legal precedents and policy proposals have emerged in response to the challenges of applying copyright to AI-generated works:

- **Thaler v. Copyright Office:** As discussed in Chapter 8, this case reaffirmed that copyright law requires human authorship, rejecting the notion of machine authorship. However, the case has prompted discussions about the need for legislative change to address the realities of AI-generated content.

- **Proposals for Legislative Reform:** Various policy proposals have been put forward to adapt copyright law to AI-generated works:
  - **WIPO's Ongoing Work:** The World Intellectual Property Organization (WIPO) has begun examining how international copyright laws could be adapted to account for AI-generated works, potentially through new treaties or guidelines that address machine authorship.
  - **National Legislative Initiatives:** Some countries, like the United Kingdom and Australia, are exploring legal reforms to recognize AI-generated works under certain conditions. These initiatives highlight the need for a balanced approach that protects both human and machine-generated creativity.
- **Creating Incentives for Responsible AI Development:** To mitigate potential negative effects, some policymakers suggest creating incentives for responsible AI development. This could involve granting copyright protection only if developers and operators adhere to ethical guidelines, such as transparency in AI training data, algorithmic accountability, and bias mitigation measures.

Moving Forward: Balancing Innovation and Protection in Copyright Law

As AI continues to play a more significant role in creative industries, policymakers and legal scholars face the challenge of balancing innovation with protection:

- **Evaluating the Need for Legal Change:** While some advocate for extending the concept of authorship to machines, others argue that the focus should remain on human creativity. Policymakers will need to carefully consider the broader implications of any changes to copyright law, taking into account economic, legal, ethical, and social factors.
- **Developing Flexible and Adaptive Legal Frameworks:** Given the rapid pace of technological advancement, there may be a need

for more flexible and adaptive legal frameworks that can evolve with the technology. This could include regular reviews of copyright laws and international cooperation to ensure consistency in the treatment of AI-generated works.

- **Encouraging Public and Stakeholder Engagement:** To develop effective legal responses, it is crucial to involve a wide range of stakeholders, including creators, developers, industry leaders, policymakers, and the public. Open dialogue and engagement can help ensure that any changes to copyright law reflect the diverse interests and values of society.

Applying Patent Laws: Protecting AI-Assisted Inventions and Patentability of Algorithms

As artificial intelligence (AI) continues to advance, its role in generating new inventions and solving complex problems has grown significantly. AI can now autonomously create inventions or assist human inventors in developing novel products, processes, and technologies. However, the application of patent laws to AI-generated or AI-assisted inventions raises complex legal and policy questions. This section explores how existing patent laws apply to AI-generated inventions, the challenges of protecting AI-assisted innovations, and the patentability of algorithms that underlie AI technologies.

Current Patent Law Framework and the Human Inventorship Requirement

Under the U.S. Patent Act, a patent is granted for new, useful, and non-obvious inventions, provided they are the product of human inventorship. The current patent law framework assumes that only human beings can be inventors, and this assumption is codified in both statutory language and case law.

- **Human Inventorship Requirement:** The U.S. Patent Act defines an "inventor" as an "individual" who conceives of the invention. The term "individual" is understood to mean a natural person, i.e., a human being. The U.S. Patent and Trademark Office (USPTO) has consistently maintained that only natural persons can be recognized as inventors on patent applications.

This interpretation was reaffirmed in cases such as *Thaler v. USPTO*, where the USPTO rejected patent applications that listed an AI as the inventor, emphasizing that the law does not permit non-human entities to be named as inventors.

- **Implications for AI-Assisted Inventions:** The human inventorship requirement presents challenges for AI-assisted inventions. When an AI system plays a substantial role in conceiving an invention, questions arise regarding who should be named as the inventor: the human who used or programmed the AI, the developer of the AI, or the AI itself. The current framework does not provide clear guidance for these scenarios, creating legal uncertainty for inventors and companies using AI.

Protecting AI-Assisted Inventions: Current Practices and Challenges

AI-assisted inventions, where AI systems are used as tools or collaborators in the inventive process, are becoming increasingly common. Protecting these inventions under existing patent laws involves several challenges:

- **Defining Human Contribution:** For an AI-assisted invention to be patentable, the human named as the inventor must have made a significant contribution to the conception of the invention. This requires demonstrating that the human had a clear role in defining the invention's novel aspects, rather than merely using the AI as a tool. However, in cases where AI systems autonomously suggest solutions or design new products with minimal human guidance, determining the extent of human contribution can be difficult.

- **Documenting the Inventive Process:** To meet the requirements of patent law, it is crucial to document the inventive process, including the role played by AI systems. This documentation should detail how the AI was used, what inputs were provided by the human inventor, and how the AI's outputs were integrated into the final invention. Proper documentation can help clarify the extent of human involvement and support the validity of the patent application. However, it also raises concerns about transparency and disclosure, particularly when proprietary AI algorithms or datasets are involved.

- **Overcoming Obviousness and Non-Obviousness Standards:** Patent law requires that an invention be non-obvious, meaning that it must not be an obvious improvement to someone skilled in the art. AI-assisted inventions may face challenges in meeting this standard, especially if the AI used to develop the invention is widely accessible or if the AI's capabilities are considered common knowledge. For example, if an AI uses a known algorithm to generate a new design, patent examiners may question whether the resulting invention is truly non-obvious.

Patentability of AI Algorithms: Protecting the Core Technologies Behind AI

Another important aspect of applying patent law to AI concerns the patentability of the algorithms and models that form the core of AI technologies. Patents on AI algorithms can provide protection for the underlying technology that enables AI systems to function, but they also raise significant legal and policy questions.

- **Current Standards for Patentability of Algorithms:** In the United States, algorithms and mathematical methods are generally considered abstract ideas and are not eligible for patent protection on their own. However, they can be patented if they are part of a concrete application or process that produces a "useful, concrete, and tangible result." The Supreme Court case *Alice Corp. v. CLS Bank International* (2014) established a two-step test for determining the patent eligibility of software and algorithms:
  - Determine whether the claims at issue are directed to a patent-ineligible concept, such as an abstract idea or law of nature.
  - If so, consider whether the claim contains an "inventive concept" sufficient to transform the abstract idea into a patent-eligible application.
- **Challenges in Patentability of AI Algorithms:** Applying the *Alice* test to AI algorithms can be challenging. Many AI

algorithms are based on well-known mathematical techniques, such as linear regression, neural networks, or clustering algorithms. To be patentable, an AI algorithm must not only demonstrate an inventive concept but also show a novel and non-obvious application of the algorithm to a specific technological problem. The requirement for novelty and non-obviousness can be difficult to meet, especially when the underlying mathematical techniques are widely known and used.

- **Patentable Subject Matter in AI:** Despite these challenges, some aspects of AI technology may still be eligible for patent protection. For example:
  - o **Innovative Training Methods:** New methods of training AI models, such as novel approaches to data augmentation or adversarial training, may qualify for patent protection if they are sufficiently innovative and non-obvious.
  - o **Specific Applications of AI:** AI technologies applied to solve specific problems in fields like healthcare, automotive, or finance may be patentable if they demonstrate a concrete and useful application. For instance, an AI system designed to detect cancer in medical images using a unique combination of algorithms and training data could be considered patentable.
  - o **Hardware and System-Level Innovations:** Innovations in AI hardware, such as specialized processors or architectures optimized for machine learning, may also be patentable, as they involve tangible technological improvements.

Potential Reforms and Adaptations to Patent Law for AI-Generated Inventions

To better accommodate AI-generated and AI-assisted inventions, several reforms and adaptations to existing patent law have been proposed:

- **Recognizing AI as Co-Inventor:** One proposed reform is to allow AI to be recognized as a co-inventor alongside human inventors. This approach would acknowledge the role of AI systems in generating inventions while maintaining a human link for legal and administrative purposes. The human co-inventor would be responsible for managing the patent and ensuring compliance with legal requirements. However, this would require legislative changes to redefine "inventor" and establish criteria for AI inventorship.

- **Creating a New Legal Framework for AI-Generated Inventions:** Another approach is to develop a new legal framework specifically for AI-generated inventions. This framework could include a new category of patents for inventions created autonomously by AI, with different rules for inventorship, ownership, and duration of protection. Such a framework could provide clarity and certainty for inventors, companies, and patent examiners, but it would require substantial legal and regulatory changes.

- **Clarifying the Patent Eligibility of AI Algorithms:** To address the challenges of patenting AI algorithms, policymakers could provide clearer guidelines on what constitutes an "inventive concept" under the *Alice* test. This could involve defining specific criteria for evaluating the patentability of AI-related inventions, such as novel combinations of algorithms, innovative applications, or unique training methods. Clearer guidelines could help reduce uncertainty and promote innovation in the AI field.

- **Encouraging Disclosure and Transparency in AI Patents:** Patent law could be adapted to encourage greater disclosure and transparency in AI-related patents. This could involve requiring applicants to provide detailed explanations of how their AI technologies work, including descriptions of the training data, algorithms, and decision-making processes used. Enhanced disclosure requirements could help ensure that patents provide meaningful information to the public and prevent overly broad or vague claims.

Balancing Innovation and Access in AI Patent Law

Any changes to patent law to accommodate AI-generated inventions must strike a balance between encouraging innovation and ensuring fair access to AI technologies:

- **Incentivizing Innovation:** Patent protection is designed to incentivize innovation by granting inventors exclusive rights to their creations. Extending patent protection to AI-assisted inventions could encourage investment in AI research and development, fostering technological advancement across various industries.
- **Avoiding Over-Monopolization:** At the same time, policymakers must consider the risk of over-monopolization if patent protection is too broad or restrictive. Patenting foundational AI algorithms or techniques could hinder competition and limit access to essential technologies, slowing innovation in the broader field.
- **Ensuring Flexibility and Adaptability:** Given the rapid pace of AI development, any legal reforms should be flexible and adaptable to changing technologies and market conditions. Policymakers should consider creating mechanisms for regular review and revision of AI-related patent laws to ensure they remain relevant and effective.

Moving Forward: Legal and Policy Considerations for AI-Related Patents

Moving forward, the legal community, patent offices, and policymakers must address several key considerations to develop a balanced approach to AI-related patents:

- **Engaging Stakeholders:** Engaging a wide range of stakeholders, including inventors, developers, companies, legal experts, and the public, is essential to understanding the full range of interests and concerns related to AI-generated inventions.
- **Monitoring International Developments:** Given the global nature of AI technologies, it is crucial to monitor and coordinate with international developments in patent law. Harmonizing patent standards and practices across jurisdictions could help create a more predictable and fair environment for AI innovation worldwide.
- **Exploring Ethical Implications:** Finally, policymakers should consider the ethical implications of extending patent protection

to AI-generated inventions. This includes assessing the potential impacts on human inventors, the distribution of economic benefits, and the broader societal implications of granting exclusive rights to AI-created innovations.

Trademarks and Design Protectionfor AI-Generated Works

Trademarks and Design: Use of AI-Generated Trademarks and Protection of Algorithm-Created "Trade Dress"

As AI technologies advance, their use in creating distinctive brand elements, such as trademarks, logos, and designs, is becoming more common. The application of AI to generate trademarks and trade dress — the visual appearance of products or packaging — raises new questions about how these elements are protected under existing trademark and design laws. This section explores the challenges and considerations involved in using AI-generated trademarks, protecting algorithm-created trade dress, and adapting existing legal frameworks to address these emerging issues.

Understanding Trademarks and Trade Dress in the Context of AI

Trademarks are words, names, symbols, designs, or any combination thereof used in commerce to identify and distinguish the goods or services of one entity from those of others. Trademarks serve as a source identifier, ensuring that consumers can associate a particular mark with a specific provider of goods or services.

Trade Dress refers to the visual appearance of a product or its packaging that indicates the source of the product to consumers. Trade dress can include aspects like shape, color, graphics, or even the configuration of a product. To be protected under U.S. trademark law, trade dress must be distinctive and have acquired secondary meaning, indicating that consumers associate it with a particular source.

- **AI-Generated Trademarks:** As businesses increasingly use AI tools to generate logos, slogans, brand names, and other trademarks, questions arise about who owns these AI-created marks and whether they are eligible for protection under existing laws.

- **Algorithm-Created Trade Dress:** Similarly, AI algorithms can design the overall look and feel of a product's packaging or shape, leading to questions about how these AI-generated designs are protected and who owns the rights to these visual elements.

Protecting AI-Generated Trademarks: Legal Considerations and Challenges

Trademarks generated by AI raise several legal considerations and challenges regarding ownership, distinctiveness, and use in commerce.

- **Ownership of AI-Generated Trademarks:** The question of ownership is central to the protection of AI-generated trademarks. Under current U.S. trademark law, a trademark must be used in commerce by a person or entity to qualify for protection. The Lanham Act, which governs trademark law in the U.S., assumes that a trademark is created and used by a human or legal entity (such as a corporation) to identify its goods or services.
  - o **Attributing Ownership to the AI User or Operator:** One approach is to attribute ownership of the AI-generated trademark to the person or entity that uses or operates the AI system. This aligns with the principle that trademarks are intended to serve as source identifiers, and it recognizes the commercial use and intent behind the creation of the mark. However, this could lead to disputes when multiple parties are involved in developing or deploying the AI system.
  - o **Challenges with Autonomous AI Systems:** When trademarks are created autonomously by AI without specific human input, the question of ownership becomes more complex. If no direct human author can be identified, it may be challenging to determine who holds the rights to the AI-generated trademark. This could lead to legal uncertainty and hinder the registration and protection of such marks.
- **Distinctiveness and Registrability of AI-Generated Trademarks:** To qualify for trademark protection, a mark must

be distinctive. Distinctiveness can be inherent (when a mark is unique and easily recognizable) or acquired (when a mark gains distinctiveness through use in commerce).

- o **Assessing Distinctiveness in AI-Generated Marks:** Determining whether an AI-generated trademark is inherently distinctive may be challenging, especially if the AI's algorithms use generic or common design elements from its training data. For example, if an AI system generates a logo that closely resembles existing marks, it may not qualify for trademark protection due to a lack of distinctiveness or because it could cause consumer confusion.

- o **Demonstrating Use in Commerce:** For a trademark to be registered, it must be used in commerce to identify the source of goods or services. For AI-generated marks, proving use in commerce may involve showing that a human entity actively deployed the mark in the marketplace. This raises questions about whether AI-created trademarks, especially those produced autonomously, can meet the "use in commerce" requirement under existing trademark laws.

- • **Preventing Consumer Confusion and Fraud:** One of the primary purposes of trademark law is to prevent consumer confusion about the source of goods or services. The use of AI-generated marks could complicate this goal if the AI system inadvertently creates marks similar to existing trademarks, leading to potential confusion among consumers. Moreover, there are concerns that AI could be used to generate misleading or fraudulent marks, further complicating enforcement efforts.

Protecting Algorithm-Created Trade Dress: Challenges and Legal Implications

AI-generated trade dress, such as the visual design of products or packaging, introduces unique challenges in determining the scope of protection and ownership under current trademark and design laws.

- • **Defining and Proving Trade Dress Created by AI:** To be protected as trade dress, a design must be distinctive and non-functional. This means it must serve as a source identifier and not merely provide a utilitarian function.

- o **Distinctiveness of AI-Created Trade Dress:** Just like AI-generated trademarks, algorithm-created trade dress must be distinctive to qualify for protection. If an AI system generates a product design that resembles existing designs or lacks unique elements, it may not be considered distinctive. Additionally, proving that an AI-generated trade dress has acquired secondary meaning — where consumers associate the design with a particular source — could be challenging if the design is not used consistently in commerce by a single entity.

- o **Non-Functionality Requirement:** The non-functionality requirement stipulates that trade dress protection cannot be granted for features that are essential to the use or purpose of a product or affect its cost or quality. AI-generated designs that improve functionality or efficiency may be excluded from trade dress protection, even if they have unique visual elements.

- **Ownership of AI-Created Trade Dress:** Similar to trademarks, the ownership of trade dress created by AI is unclear. Current law presumes that trade dress rights belong to the person or entity that uses the design in commerce to identify their products. However, if AI autonomously creates trade dress, determining the rightful owner becomes problematic, especially when the design is generated with minimal or no human input.

- **Potential for Confusion or Infringement:** There is also a risk that AI-created trade dress could infringe on existing protected designs, especially if the AI's training data includes elements from other protected trade dress or if the AI inadvertently creates designs that resemble existing products. This could lead to increased litigation and challenges in enforcing trade dress rights.

Adapting Existing Laws and Regulations to Address AI-Generated Trademarks and Trade Dress

To effectively protect AI-generated trademarks and trade dress, several adaptations to existing laws and regulations may be necessary:

- **Clarifying Ownership Rules:** Legislators could amend trademark and design laws to clarify the rules around ownership of AI-generated marks and trade dress. For example, the law could specify that ownership resides with the user or operator of the AI system, or it could provide guidelines for shared ownership in cases where multiple parties are involved in the creation and commercialization of the mark or design.

- **Establishing Criteria for Distinctiveness and Use in Commerce:** Policymakers could develop specific criteria for assessing the distinctiveness of AI-generated trademarks and trade dress. This could include guidance on how to evaluate marks created using AI tools, taking into account factors such as the originality of the design elements and the intent behind the mark's use. Additionally, clearer rules on what constitutes "use in commerce" for AI-generated marks could help resolve ambiguities and promote consistency in trademark registration and enforcement.

- **Encouraging Transparency and Ethical Use of AI in Branding:** To prevent consumer confusion and fraud, regulatory bodies like the U.S. Patent and Trademark Office (USPTO) could encourage transparency in the use of AI for branding purposes. This could involve requiring applicants to disclose the use of AI tools in generating trademarks or trade dress and ensuring that AI-generated marks comply with ethical guidelines to prevent deception or misuse.

- **Creating New Categories for AI-Generated Designs:** Another approach is to create new categories or subclasses for AI-generated designs under existing trademark and design registration systems. These categories could have their own rules for distinctiveness, ownership, and enforcement, tailored to the unique characteristics of AI-generated content.

Implications for Businesses and the Future of Branding with AI

As AI-generated trademarks and trade dress become more common, businesses and brand owners must navigate the evolving legal landscape and consider the implications for their branding strategies:

- **Leveraging AI for Creative Innovation:** Businesses can use AI to enhance creativity and innovation in branding, creating unique marks and designs that capture consumer attention and differentiate their products. However, they must be aware of the legal risks and challenges involved in protecting AI-generated content and ensuring compliance with trademark and design laws.
- **Navigating Ownership and Enforcement Complexities:** Companies will need to carefully manage ownership rights for AI-generated trademarks and trade dress, particularly in collaborative environments where multiple parties contribute to the development of AI tools. Clear agreements and contractual arrangements can help clarify rights and responsibilities, reducing the risk of disputes.
- **Adapting to Legal Reforms and New Regulatory Frameworks:** As laws and regulations evolve to address AI-generated content, businesses must stay informed about changes and adapt their strategies accordingly. This may involve working with legal experts to ensure that AI-generated trademarks and trade dress are registered, protected, and enforced effectively.

Moving Forward: Legal and Policy Considerations for AI-Generated Trademarks and Trade Dress

To address the challenges of protecting AI-generated trademarks and trade dress, policymakers, legal experts, and businesses should consider the following:

- **Promoting International Harmonization:** Given the global nature of branding and trade, there is a need for international cooperation to harmonize the rules governing AI-generated trademarks and trade dress. Organizations such as the World

201

Intellectual Property Organization (WIPO) can play a key role in developing consistent standards and guidelines.

- **Encouraging Ethical AI Use in Branding:** Regulatory bodies should encourage the ethical use of AI in branding by promoting transparency, accountability, and fairness. This includes developing guidelines for the responsible use of AI in creating trademarks and trade dress, ensuring that AI-generated marks do not mislead or confuse consumers.
- **Exploring New Legal Frameworks:** Finally, there may be a need to explore new legal frameworks or categories specifically for AI-generated trademarks and trade dress. Such frameworks could provide greater clarity and protection for businesses using AI in their branding efforts, while also balancing the interests of consumers and other stakeholders.

Innovative Proposals and Future Models for Legal Protection (7-8 pages)

As AI continues to transform creative industries and generate novel works across various mediums, there is a growing need for innovative legal frameworks that can adequately protect these creations. The existing intellectual property laws, designed primarily for human authorship, struggle to accommodate the unique characteristics of AI-generated works. This section explores several forward-looking proposals and models for the legal protection of AI-generated content, focusing on creating new copyright categories, establishing international standards, and developing novel contractual and licensing frameworks.

Creating New Copyright Categories for AI-Generated Works: The "AI Authorship Unit" Model

One innovative proposal to address the challenges of protecting AI-generated works is the creation of new copyright categories specifically designed for these types of content. The "AI Authorship Unit" (AAU) model represents a novel approach to recognizing and managing the rights associated with works generated by AI systems.

Defining the "AI Authorship Unit" Model

The "AI Authorship Unit" model proposes establishing a new category within copyright law that grants a distinct form of protection to works generated by AI. Under this model, an AI system, along with its human developers, operators, or owners, would be recognized as a unitary entity for the purposes of copyright.

- **Characteristics of the AI Authorship Unit:**
  - **Hybrid Entity Structure:** The AAU model treats the AI system and the associated human stakeholders (developers, owners, or operators) as a hybrid entity. This entity would collectively hold the rights to any works generated by the AI, balancing the need for human oversight with the recognition of the AI's role in the creative process.
  - **AI as a Co-Creator:** In this model, the AI system itself is not considered the sole author but rather a co-creator. The human stakeholders would manage and exploit the rights, while the AI's contribution is legally acknowledged, ensuring that the unique aspects of machine-generated creativity are protected.
  - **Limited Duration of Protection:** To address concerns about perpetual monopolies on creative works, the AAU model could provide a shorter duration of copyright protection for AI-generated works compared to human-authored works. This limited duration would recognize the reduced level of human creativity and ensure a balance between protection and public access.

Benefits of the AI Authorship Unit Model

- **Encourages Innovation and Investment:** By providing a clear legal framework for the protection of AI-generated works, the AAU model would encourage innovation and investment in AI technologies. Companies and developers would be incentivized to create and deploy AI systems capable of generating valuable content, knowing that their creations would be legally protected.
- **Balances Human Oversight with Machine Creativity:** The model acknowledges both human and machine contributions,

ensuring that human stakeholders remain accountable for the works generated by their AI systems. This balance helps maintain ethical standards and ensures that AI is used responsibly in creative industries.

- **Reduces Legal Uncertainty:** The AAU model would provide greater clarity and predictability in the legal treatment of AI-generated works. It would create a specific category for these works, reducing ambiguity about their eligibility for protection and the rights of various stakeholders.

Challenges and Considerations for the AI Authorship Unit Model

- **Defining the Scope of Protection:** One of the challenges of the AAU model is determining the scope of protection for AI-generated works. Policymakers would need to define what constitutes a sufficient level of human oversight and contribution to qualify for protection under this model. Additionally, the criteria for assessing the originality and creativity of AI-generated works would need to be clearly established.

- **Managing Multiple Stakeholders:** The AAU model involves multiple stakeholders (developers, owners, operators), which could lead to conflicts over ownership, rights management, and profit distribution. Clear guidelines and mechanisms would be needed to resolve disputes and ensure fair treatment of all parties involved.

- **International Harmonization:** Given the global nature of creative industries and AI technologies, international cooperation would be necessary to implement the AAU model effectively. Aligning different jurisdictions on the recognition and protection of AI-generated works would require significant negotiation and consensus-building.

International Framework: Proposals for Global Standards on Intellectual Property for Machine-Generated Works (e.g., WIPO and W3C)

To ensure consistent and effective protection of AI-generated works across borders, there is a growing call for an international framework that establishes global standards on intellectual property for machine-generated content. Organizations like the World Intellectual Property Organization (WIPO) and the World Wide Web Consortium (W3C) are at the forefront of these efforts.

The Need for an International Framework

- **Cross-Border Nature of AI-Generated Works:** AI-generated works, such as digital art, software, and music, can easily cross borders through online platforms and international distribution channels. This global reach creates a need for harmonized IP standards that can provide consistent protection and enforcement across jurisdictions.
- **Avoiding Fragmentation of IP Laws:** Without international standards, countries may develop divergent laws regarding the protection of AI-generated works, leading to legal uncertainty and potential conflicts. A fragmented legal landscape could create barriers to trade, hinder innovation, and complicate enforcement efforts.

Proposals for Global Standards by International Organizations

- **World Intellectual Property Organization (WIPO):** WIPO has initiated discussions on the challenges and opportunities presented by AI for intellectual property law. WIPO's potential role in developing global standards includes:
  - **Creating Model Laws and Guidelines:** WIPO could develop model laws or guidelines that countries can adopt or adapt to their national contexts. These models would provide a baseline for protecting AI-generated works, covering aspects such as authorship, ownership, duration of protection, and enforcement.
  - **Facilitating International Agreements:** WIPO could facilitate international agreements or treaties specifically addressing AI-generated works. Such agreements could establish common principles for IP protection, dispute resolution, and cross-border enforcement.
  - **Promoting Capacity Building:** WIPO could support capacity building in member countries by providing training,

resources, and technical assistance to help them understand and implement new IP standards for AI-generated works.

- **World Wide Web Consortium (W3C):** As a global standards organization focused on web technologies, W3C could play a role in establishing technical standards and protocols for the use of AI in creative content:
  - **Developing Technical Protocols:** W3C could develop technical standards that ensure transparency and traceability in the use of AI tools for generating creative works. These standards could help address issues such as attribution, data provenance, and the detection of AI-generated content.
  - **Ensuring Interoperability:** W3C could work with other international bodies to ensure that technical standards for AI-generated works are interoperable across different platforms and technologies, facilitating smoother cross-border trade and collaboration.

Benefits and Challenges of an International Framework

- **Benefits:**
  - **Consistent Protection Across Jurisdictions:** A global framework would provide consistent protection for AI-generated works, reducing legal uncertainties and promoting international trade and cooperation.
  - **Facilitating Innovation and Collaboration:** By establishing common standards, an international framework would encourage innovation and collaboration across borders, allowing creators, developers, and businesses to operate with greater confidence and clarity.
  - **Addressing Ethical and Policy Concerns:** International standards could also address ethical and policy concerns related to AI-generated works, such as ensuring fairness, transparency, and accountability in the use of AI tools.

- **Challenges:**
  - **Diverse Legal Systems and Interests:** Reaching consensus on global standards may be challenging due to the diverse

legal systems, cultural values, and economic interests of different countries. Some countries may prioritize strong IP protections to encourage innovation, while others may favor more open access to creative works.

- o **Ensuring Compliance and Enforcement:** Even with international standards, ensuring compliance and enforcement across jurisdictions can be difficult. Effective mechanisms for dispute resolution and cooperation between countries would be necessary to make the framework work in practice.

Contractual and Licensing Models: Smart Contracts on Blockchain, Limited Use Licenses, and Marketability of AI Works

Beyond adapting existing legal frameworks, innovative contractual and licensing models can provide flexible and dynamic solutions for managing the rights and uses of AI-generated works. These models leverage emerging technologies like blockchain and explore new ways to license and commercialize AI-generated content.

Smart Contracts on Blockchain

- **Definition and Functionality:** Smart contracts are self-executing contracts with the terms of the agreement directly written into code and stored on a blockchain. These contracts automatically execute actions (such as payments or transfers of rights) when predefined conditions are met.
  - o **Application for AI-Generated Works:** Smart contracts could be used to manage the licensing, distribution, and monetization of AI-generated works. For example, a smart contract could automatically distribute royalties to stakeholders (developers, users, or data providers) based on predefined revenue-sharing agreements.
  - o **Advantages of Using Smart Contracts:**
    - ■ **Transparency and Trust:** Smart contracts provide a transparent and tamper-proof record of transactions, enhancing trust between parties.

207

- **Efficiency and Automation:** The automated nature of smart contracts reduces the need for intermediaries, lowering transaction costs and speeding up processes like licensing and payment distribution.

Limited Use Licenses for AI Works

- **Definition and Purpose:** Limited use licenses provide a flexible approach to managing the rights of AI-generated works by granting specific rights to use the content under certain conditions. These licenses can be tailored to fit different use cases, such as non-commercial use, time-limited use, or use in specific geographic regions.

  o **Application for AI-Generated Works:** Limited use licenses can offer a more nuanced approach to licensing AI-generated content. For instance, an artist or developer might grant a limited license to use an AI-generated image for a specific marketing campaign, while retaining the right to use the image for other purposes.
  o **Advantages of Limited Use Licenses:**
    - **Customizability:** Licenses can be customized to fit the needs and preferences of both the rights holder and the user.
    - **Marketability:** By offering various levels of rights and permissions, limited use licenses can increase the marketability of AI-generated works and provide more revenue opportunities for creators and developers.

Marketability of AI Works Through New Licensing Models

- **Developing New Licensing Platforms:** To enhance the marketability of AI-generated works, new licensing platforms and marketplaces could be developed specifically for AI-generated content. These platforms could offer tools for rights management, pricing, and distribution, making it easier for creators and users to find and license AI-generated works.
- **Facilitating Access and Innovation:** New licensing models could help democratize access to AI-generated works by offering

flexible pricing and licensing options. This could encourage innovation and creativity by making it easier for small businesses, artists, and startups to use AI-generated content without needing to navigate complex legal frameworks.

Benefits and Challenges of New Contractual and Licensing Models

- **Benefits:**
  - **Flexibility and Adaptability:** These models offer flexible and adaptable ways to manage the rights of AI-generated works, accommodating diverse use cases and preferences.
  - **Enhanced Market Efficiency:** By reducing transaction costs and providing clear terms, these models can enhance market efficiency and facilitate the commercial exploitation of AI-generated content.
  - **Leveraging Technology for Legal Solutions:** The use of technologies like blockchain can enhance trust, transparency, and security in licensing arrangements, reducing the risk of disputes and unauthorized use.

- **Challenges:**
  - **Regulatory and Legal Barriers:** Implementing these models may require overcoming regulatory and legal barriers, such as uncertainty about the enforceability of smart contracts in different jurisdictions.
  - **Technical Complexity:** Developing and maintaining new platforms and technologies, such as blockchain-based licensing systems, may involve technical challenges and costs.
  - **Adoption and Acceptance:** Encouraging widespread adoption of new contractual and licensing models may require education, outreach, and incentives to help stakeholders understand and embrace these approaches.

Moving Forward: Embracing Innovation in Legal Protection for AI Works

To effectively protect and manage AI-generated works, stakeholders should consider the following:

- **Promoting Technological Integration in Legal Frameworks:** Policymakers and legal experts should explore ways to integrate emerging technologies, such as blockchain and smart contracts, into legal frameworks for intellectual property.
- **Fostering Collaboration and Innovation:** Collaboration between international organizations, governments, businesses, and creators is essential to develop innovative solutions that balance protection with access and encourage responsible AI use.
- **Adapting to Evolving Needs:** As AI technologies and creative industries evolve, legal frameworks and licensing models must remain flexible and adaptable to address new challenges and opportunities.

Alternatives to Traditional Legal Protection: Innovations and Creative Approaches (6-7 pages)

As the legal community grapples with the challenges posed by AI-generated works, many stakeholders are exploring alternatives to traditional intellectual property (IP) protections. These alternatives seek to balance the need for protection with the promotion of innovation, collaboration, and public access. One of the most promising approaches involves using open source licenses and Creative Commons licenses to manage AI-generated content. This section examines the potential benefits and drawbacks of applying these licensing models to AI-generated works, highlighting their advantages, limitations, and implications for the future of creative industries.

Open Source Licenses and Creative Commons for AI Works: Benefits and Drawbacks

Open source licenses and Creative Commons licenses are widely used in software, creative arts, and academic fields to promote sharing, collaboration, and innovation. Applying these models to AI-generated works could provide new opportunities for creators, developers, and users while also presenting unique challenges and trade-offs.

Understanding Open Source and Creative Commons Licenses

- **Open Source Licenses:** Open source licenses are legal instruments that allow software and other works to be freely used, modified, and distributed by anyone, provided they comply with certain conditions set by the license. Common open source licenses include the MIT License, the GNU General Public License (GPL), and the Apache License. These licenses promote transparency, collaboration, and community-driven development.

- **Creative Commons Licenses:** Creative Commons (CC) licenses offer a flexible range of protections and freedoms for authors and users. There are several types of CC licenses, each with different levels of restriction, ranging from the most permissive (CC BY, which only requires attribution) to more restrictive licenses (CC BY-NC-ND, which allows use with attribution but restricts commercial use and the creation of derivative works). Creative Commons licenses are often used for creative content, such as text, images, music, and videos.

Benefits of Applying Open Source and Creative Commons Licenses to AI-Generated Works

Applying open source and Creative Commons licenses to AI-generated works offers several benefits:

- **Promoting Collaboration and Innovation:** Open source and Creative Commons licenses encourage collaboration by allowing creators, developers, and users to freely share, modify, and build upon AI-generated content. This can lead to new innovations and creative solutions, as diverse stakeholders contribute their expertise and ideas.

- **Increasing Access and Distribution:** These licensing models help increase access to AI-generated works by making them available to a broader audience. They can reduce barriers to entry for smaller companies, independent creators, and educational institutions, enabling them to use and adapt AI-generated content without needing to navigate complex or costly licensing agreements.

- **Fostering Transparency and Trust:** By making AI-generated works openly available, these licenses promote transparency in the creation and use of AI technologies. Open access to AI models, training data, and outputs allows researchers, developers, and the public to scrutinize, understand, and improve these systems, fostering trust in their use.

- **Supporting Ethical AI Development:** Open source and Creative Commons licensing can help ensure ethical use of AI-generated works by making them accessible for non-commercial, educational, and humanitarian purposes. This approach aligns with broader efforts to promote socially beneficial uses of AI and prevent the concentration of AI capabilities in the hands of a few entities.

- **Lowering Costs and Reducing Legal Complexity:** For creators and developers, using open source or Creative Commons licenses can lower the costs and complexity associated with traditional IP protection. These licenses provide a standardized legal framework for sharing and collaboration, reducing the need for bespoke contracts and legal negotiations.

Drawbacks and Challenges of Applying Open Source and Creative Commons Licenses to AI-Generated Works

While open source and Creative Commons licenses offer many advantages, there are also significant drawbacks and challenges to their use for AI-generated works:

- **Lack of Commercial Incentives:** One of the primary criticisms of open source and Creative Commons licensing is that they may provide insufficient commercial incentives for creators and developers. Without the exclusive rights offered by traditional IP protections, there may be less motivation to invest time, resources, and effort into developing high-quality AI-generated content. This could slow down innovation in areas that require substantial investment.

- **Risk of Misuse and Exploitation:** Open licenses can increase the risk of misuse or exploitation of AI-generated works. Without adequate controls, bad actors may use open-source AI models or datasets to develop harmful applications, such as surveillance technologies or biased decision-making tools. While licenses can include clauses that prohibit certain uses, enforcing these restrictions can be challenging.
- **Limited Control Over Derivative Works:** Open source and Creative Commons licenses often allow for the creation of derivative works, which can lead to unintended uses or modifications of the original content. Creators may lose control over how their works are adapted or used, potentially resulting in reputational harm or association with objectionable content.
- **Potential for Fragmentation and Forking:** In the context of open source software, "forking" occurs when developers take the original source code and modify it to create a new, separate version. While this can promote innovation, it can also lead to fragmentation, where multiple incompatible versions of the same AI model or content exist. This fragmentation can reduce interoperability and complicate collaboration.
- **Enforcement Challenges:** Enforcing open source or Creative Commons licenses can be difficult, particularly across jurisdictions with different legal systems and interpretations. Creators may struggle to ensure compliance with license terms, especially if their works are used in ways that violate the license conditions, such as for commercial purposes without permission.

Examples of Applying Open Source and Creative Commons Licenses to AI-Generated Works

Several organizations and projects have successfully applied open source and Creative Commons licenses to AI-generated works:

- **OpenAI's GPT Models:** OpenAI initially released earlier versions of its GPT models under open licenses to promote research and development in natural language processing (NLP). By making the models available for public use, OpenAI encouraged collaboration and innovation while also fostering transparency in AI development.

- **Creative Commons Licenses for AI Art:** Some artists and creators have chosen to license their AI-generated artworks under Creative Commons licenses. This allows others to share, adapt, and build upon the original works while maintaining certain rights, such as requiring attribution or restricting commercial use.

- **Open Source AI Projects and Libraries:** Many AI tools, libraries, and frameworks, such as TensorFlow (Google) and PyTorch (Facebook), are released under open source licenses. These licenses have enabled widespread adoption, adaptation, and improvement of these tools by developers and researchers worldwide, accelerating AI innovation.

Balancing the Benefits and Drawbacks: Hybrid Approaches and Creative Solutions

To balance the benefits and drawbacks of open source and Creative Commons licensing for AI-generated works, stakeholders could consider hybrid approaches and creative solutions:

- **Dual Licensing Models:** Creators could use dual licensing models that offer both open licenses and traditional IP protections. For example, a developer might release an AI model under an open source license for non-commercial use while retaining the rights for commercial exploitation. This approach allows for both collaboration and monetization, depending on the use case.

- **Adopting Ethical Open Source Standards:** To mitigate risks of misuse, organizations could adopt ethical open source standards that include explicit clauses prohibiting harmful or unethical uses of AI-generated content. These standards could be developed by industry groups, non-profits, or international bodies to promote responsible AI development.

- **Creating Commons-Based Revenue Models:** Innovative business models, such as the "Creative Commons Plus" (CC+) license, could be adapted for AI-generated works. The CC+ model allows creators to offer their works for free under a

Creative Commons license while providing additional services or rights (such as commercial use) for a fee. This approach combines the benefits of open access with opportunities for revenue generation.

Moving Forward: Considerations for Implementing Open Source and Creative Commons Licensing for AI Works

To implement open source and Creative Commons licensing for AI-generated works effectively, stakeholders should consider the following:

- **Educating Stakeholders on Licensing Options:** Providing education and resources for creators, developers, and users on the various licensing options available and their implications can help stakeholders make informed decisions about how to license and use AI-generated content.
- **Collaborating on Best Practices:** Encouraging collaboration among creators, developers, legal experts, and policymakers to establish best practices for licensing AI-generated works can help address challenges and promote responsible use.
- **Exploring New Models and Technologies:** As the landscape for AI-generated works evolves, stakeholders should remain open to new models and technologies, such as blockchain-based licensing or smart contracts, that could provide innovative solutions for managing rights and licenses.

Alternative Registration Systems: Blockchain as a Mechanism for Proof of Authorship and Distribution

Blockchain technology, with its decentralized and immutable nature, presents a novel mechanism for establishing proof of authorship and managing the distribution of AI-generated works. As an alternative to traditional registration systems like national copyright offices, blockchain offers a transparent, secure, and efficient way to record ownership and track the use of creative content. This section explores the benefits, challenges, and potential applications of blockchain as a mechanism for proving authorship and managing the distribution of AI-generated works.

Understanding Blockchain Technology in the Context of IP Protection

Blockchain is a distributed ledger technology that securely records transactions across a network of computers. Each transaction is verified by network participants and added to a "block," which is then linked to previous blocks, forming a "chain." Once added, the information on a blockchain is nearly impossible to alter, providing a secure and tamper-proof record.

- **Decentralization:** Unlike traditional centralized databases, blockchain does not rely on a single entity for verification. Instead, multiple participants (nodes) validate transactions, making the system more resilient to tampering and fraud.
- **Immutability:** The data stored on a blockchain is immutable, meaning it cannot be easily changed or deleted. This feature provides a reliable way to prove that a particular piece of content existed at a specific time and was attributed to a particular author or creator.
- **Transparency:** Blockchain transactions are visible to all participants, offering transparency in how works are registered, licensed, and used. This visibility helps build trust among creators, users, and other stakeholders.

Using Blockchain for Proof of Authorship

Blockchain can be used as an alternative mechanism to establish proof of authorship for AI-generated works, providing a secure and transparent way to document the creation and ownership of digital content.

- **Timestamping and Verification:** Creators can use blockchain to timestamp their AI-generated works, creating a verifiable record of when the work was created and by whom. By registering the work on a blockchain, creators can provide a proof of authorship that is secure, time-stamped, and easily accessible. This can be especially useful in disputes over ownership or priority of creation.
- **Smart Contracts for Automatic Rights Management:** Blockchain can facilitate the use of smart contracts — self-

executing contracts with terms directly written into code — to manage the rights associated with AI-generated works. For example, a smart contract could automatically enforce licensing terms, distribute royalties, or trigger payments when a work is used in a specific way. This reduces the need for intermediaries and enhances the efficiency of rights management.

- **Preventing Unauthorized Use:** By providing a transparent and immutable record of authorship, blockchain can help prevent unauthorized use or copying of AI-generated works. If a creator registers their work on a blockchain, they can prove ownership if a dispute arises, deterring potential infringers and protecting their rights.

Blockchain for Distribution and Licensing of AI-Generated Works

Blockchain technology can also play a significant role in the distribution and licensing of AI-generated works, providing a secure and efficient mechanism for managing digital rights and transactions.

- **Decentralized Marketplaces:** Blockchain enables the creation of decentralized marketplaces for AI-generated works, where creators can directly connect with buyers, licensees, and users. These marketplaces can facilitate peer-to-peer transactions, reducing transaction costs and allowing creators to retain a larger share of the revenue.

- **Tokenization of Creative Works:** Blockchain can support the tokenization of AI-generated works, turning them into unique digital assets (tokens) that can be bought, sold, or traded on blockchain networks. Each token represents ownership or rights to a specific work, and its provenance can be tracked transparently. This approach is already being explored in the context of Non-Fungible Tokens (NFTs), which have gained popularity for digital art, music, and other creative content.

- **Automated Licensing and Royalty Distribution:** Smart contracts on a blockchain can automate licensing processes and royalty payments. For instance, when an AI-generated work is used or sold, the smart contract can automatically execute the agreed-upon licensing terms and distribute royalties to the relevant parties. This eliminates delays and reduces administrative costs associated with traditional licensing models.

Benefits of Using Blockchain for AI-Generated Works

Blockchain technology offers several benefits as an alternative registration and distribution mechanism for AI-generated works:

- **Enhanced Security and Trust:** The decentralized and immutable nature of blockchain provides a high level of security against fraud, tampering, and unauthorized alterations. Creators and users can trust that the records of authorship and transactions are accurate and reliable.

- **Greater Transparency and Accountability:** Blockchain's transparency allows all participants to view the history of transactions and the chain of ownership. This transparency can reduce disputes, enhance accountability, and foster a more trustworthy environment for licensing and distributing AI-generated works.

- **Reduced Intermediary Costs:** By enabling direct peer-to-peer transactions, blockchain reduces the need for intermediaries such as copyright offices, licensing agencies, or collection societies. This can lower transaction costs, increase efficiency, and allow creators to retain a greater share of the revenue generated from their works.

- **Flexible and Automated Rights Management:** Smart contracts provide a flexible and automated way to manage rights and distribute royalties. This reduces administrative burdens and ensures that creators are compensated fairly and promptly.

Challenges and Limitations of Using Blockchain for IP Protection

While blockchain offers many benefits, there are also challenges and limitations to its use as a mechanism for proving authorship and managing AI-generated works:

- **Legal Recognition and Enforceability:** One of the main challenges is the lack of legal recognition and enforceability of blockchain-based records in many jurisdictions. While blockchain provides a technological solution for proving authorship, it may not be accepted as definitive proof in courts or by regulatory bodies that rely on traditional evidence standards.

- **Scalability and Energy Consumption:** Blockchain networks, especially those using proof-of-work consensus mechanisms, can face scalability issues and consume significant amounts of energy. This raises concerns about the environmental impact and the ability of blockchain systems to handle large volumes of transactions efficiently.
- **Data Privacy and Compliance:** Blockchain's transparency can also pose challenges for data privacy and compliance with regulations like the General Data Protection Regulation (GDPR) in the European Union. Because blockchain records are immutable and publicly accessible, they may conflict with data protection laws that require the ability to erase personal data upon request.
- **Complexity and Accessibility:** Blockchain technology can be complex and may require technical expertise to implement and maintain. Smaller creators or developers may lack the resources or knowledge needed to navigate blockchain-based systems, limiting its accessibility and adoption.

Examples of Blockchain Applications for IP Protection

Several initiatives and platforms have begun exploring the use of blockchain for IP protection and the distribution of AI-generated works:

- **Ascribe.io:** Ascribe is a platform that uses blockchain to register digital art and creative works, providing a proof of authorship and enabling artists to transfer and manage rights. It allows creators to timestamp their works and generate a secure record of ownership that can be verified by anyone.
- **Verisart:** Verisart offers blockchain-based certification for digital art, helping to establish provenance and authenticity. The platform allows artists to create certificates of authenticity and secure records of ownership for their works, which can be useful in protecting and managing digital content, including AI-generated art.

- **IPwe:** IPwe is a blockchain-powered platform for managing and transacting IP rights, including patents, trademarks, and copyrights. The platform uses blockchain to create a transparent and efficient marketplace for IP assets, allowing creators and owners to track and manage their rights more effectively.

Moving Forward: Integrating Blockchain with Traditional IP Systems

To maximize the benefits of blockchain for AI-generated works, stakeholders should consider integrating blockchain with existing IP systems:

- **Developing Hybrid Models:** Combining traditional IP registration systems with blockchain technology could offer a hybrid approach that leverages the strengths of both systems. For example, copyright offices could use blockchain to timestamp registrations and maintain secure digital records, enhancing the reliability and accessibility of IP databases.
- **Encouraging Legal Recognition and Standardization:** Governments and international organizations should work towards recognizing blockchain-based records as valid proof of authorship and ownership in legal proceedings. Developing standardized protocols for using blockchain in IP protection could help promote broader acceptance and interoperability across jurisdictions.
- **Fostering Collaboration and Innovation:** Collaboration between creators, developers, legal experts, and policymakers is essential to address the challenges and opportunities of using blockchain for IP protection. Ongoing dialogue and experimentation can help refine and improve blockchain applications for managing AI-generated works.

Conclusion: The Future of Blockchain in IP Protection for AI-Generated Works

Blockchain offers a promising alternative to traditional IP protection methods, providing a secure, transparent, and efficient way to prove authorship and manage the distribution of AI-generated works.

However, its success will depend on overcoming legal, technical, and practical challenges, as well as fostering collaboration among stakeholders to develop effective and sustainable solutions.

Data and Privacy-Based Protection: Using Advanced Data Masking and Anonymization Techniques to Safeguard AI

In addition to traditional intellectual property (IP) protections, data and privacy-based protection strategies are becoming increasingly important for safeguarding AI-generated works and the underlying data used to create them. Advanced data masking and anonymization techniques can help protect sensitive data, maintain privacy, and ensure the ethical use of AI. These techniques not only mitigate risks related to data breaches and unauthorized access but also support compliance with data protection laws such as the General Data Protection Regulation (GDPR). This section explores how data masking and anonymization can be used to protect AI-generated works, the benefits and challenges of these approaches, and potential future directions.

Understanding Data Masking and Anonymization Techniques

- **Data Masking:** Data masking involves altering data in such a way that it remains usable for analytical purposes but is no longer sensitive or identifiable. Techniques for data masking include replacing real data with fictional data, scrambling data values, or encrypting data. The goal is to ensure that the masked data cannot be traced back to an individual or entity while still allowing it to be used for AI training and other purposes.
- **Data Anonymization:** Data anonymization goes a step further by irreversibly transforming data so that it cannot be linked back to any individual or entity. Common anonymization techniques include generalization (reducing the precision of data), suppression (removing identifying data), and adding noise (introducing random variations). Anonymization aims to protect personal and sensitive information while allowing the data to be used for legitimate purposes.

Protecting AI-Generated Works with Data Masking and Anonymization

Advanced data masking and anonymization techniques can help protect both the AI-generated works and the underlying data that feeds AI models, addressing key privacy concerns and enhancing security.

- **Safeguarding Training Data:** AI models are often trained on vast datasets that may contain sensitive or personal information. By applying data masking and anonymization techniques, developers can reduce the risk of exposing sensitive data during training or sharing. This not only protects individuals' privacy but also ensures compliance with data protection regulations.
- **Preventing Data Leakage in AI Models:** During the training process, AI models can inadvertently learn patterns or details that could reveal sensitive information, a phenomenon known as "data leakage." Data masking and anonymization techniques can help prevent this by ensuring that the training data does not contain identifiable information that could be extracted or reconstructed by the AI model.
- **Securing AI Outputs:** In some cases, the outputs of AI models can contain information that reveals sensitive data, especially in natural language processing or image recognition tasks. Anonymization techniques can be used to sanitize AI outputs, removing any inadvertently disclosed information that could compromise privacy.

Benefits of Using Data Masking and Anonymization for AI Protection

Implementing data masking and anonymization techniques offers several benefits for protecting AI-generated works and maintaining data privacy:

- **Enhancing Compliance with Data Protection Laws:** Anonymization and masking help organizations comply with data protection laws such as the GDPR, California Consumer Privacy Act (CCPA), and others that require stringent controls over the use of personal data. By anonymizing data, organizations can reduce the risk of regulatory penalties and demonstrate a commitment to data privacy.

- **Reducing Risk of Data Breaches:** By masking or anonymizing data, organizations reduce the risk of exposing sensitive information in the event of a data breach. Since the data is rendered less identifiable, the impact of a breach is minimized, and the risk to individuals' privacy is mitigated.
- **Facilitating Secure Data Sharing and Collaboration:** Data masking and anonymization make it easier to share data securely with external partners, researchers, or collaborators without compromising privacy. This facilitates collaboration while maintaining control over sensitive information and protecting intellectual property.
- **Supporting Ethical AI Development:** Data protection techniques contribute to the ethical use of AI by ensuring that AI models are developed and deployed without compromising individuals' privacy rights. This aligns with broader ethical guidelines and frameworks for responsible AI development.

Challenges and Limitations of Data Masking and Anonymization for AI

While data masking and anonymization offer valuable protections, they also present several challenges and limitations:

- **Balancing Privacy with Data Utility:** Anonymization and masking can sometimes degrade the quality or utility of data, making it less effective for training AI models. Finding the right balance between protecting privacy and maintaining data quality is a significant challenge. Overly aggressive anonymization may strip away important details, reducing the AI model's accuracy and effectiveness.
- **Re-identification Risks:** Even with advanced anonymization techniques, there is always a risk of re-identification, especially when combined with other datasets. Sophisticated adversaries can use additional information or background knowledge to re-identify anonymized data, particularly when the data contains unique patterns or rare characteristics.

- **Complexity and Cost of Implementation:** Implementing robust data masking and anonymization techniques can be complex and costly, requiring specialized tools, expertise, and resources. Smaller organizations or individual developers may lack the capacity to implement these techniques effectively, limiting their accessibility.
- **Regulatory Ambiguities:** While anonymization is often seen as a safeguard against data protection laws, there is sometimes ambiguity about what constitutes "sufficient" anonymization. Different jurisdictions may have varying standards, making it challenging for organizations to ensure compliance across borders.

Techniques for Effective Data Masking and Anonymization in AI

Several advanced techniques can enhance the effectiveness of data masking and anonymization in protecting AI-generated works:

- **Differential Privacy:** Differential privacy adds random noise to data or results to prevent the extraction of individual information while allowing aggregate analysis. It is particularly useful in AI and machine learning, where preserving data privacy is essential without sacrificing model accuracy.
- **Synthetic Data Generation:** Synthetic data is artificially generated data that mimics the statistical properties of real data but does not contain any actual personal information. This technique can provide a safe alternative for training AI models, particularly when real data is sensitive or difficult to obtain.
- **K-Anonymity and L-Diversity:** These techniques involve modifying data to ensure that individual records cannot be distinguished from at least 'k' others or ensuring that sensitive attributes within a dataset have diverse values. K-anonymity reduces the risk of re-identification, while L-diversity adds an extra layer of protection by ensuring that data records are not easily linked to specific individuals.
- **Federated Learning:** Federated learning enables AI models to be trained across multiple decentralized devices or servers holding local data samples, without transferring the data itself.

This approach allows the use of private data for training while keeping it localized and secure, reducing the risk of data breaches and maintaining privacy.

Examples of Data Masking and Anonymization in AI Applications

- **Healthcare AI Models:** Healthcare applications often use AI to analyze patient data and provide diagnostic or treatment recommendations. To comply with data protection laws like HIPAA (Health Insurance Portability and Accountability Act), data masking and anonymization techniques are applied to de-identify patient data before it is used to train AI models.
- **Financial Services AI Models:** In financial services, AI models are used for risk assessment, fraud detection, and customer analytics. Financial institutions apply data masking and anonymization to protect sensitive customer information while maintaining data integrity for analysis and model training.
- **Natural Language Processing (NLP):** AI models for NLP tasks such as sentiment analysis, translation, or text generation often use large datasets containing personal or sensitive information. Anonymization techniques, such as redacting names or specific details, can help protect privacy while still enabling effective training and use of AI models.

Future Directions and Innovations in Data and Privacy-Based Protection for AI

As AI technologies continue to evolve, data masking and anonymization techniques will need to adapt to new challenges and requirements:

- **Developing Dynamic and Adaptive Privacy Techniques:** Future innovations may focus on creating dynamic privacy techniques that adjust the level of data masking or anonymization based on the specific use case, sensitivity of the data, and the privacy preferences of individuals.
- **Integrating Privacy-by-Design Principles:** Organizations should integrate privacy-by-design principles into AI development, ensuring that privacy considerations are embedded

throughout the lifecycle of AI systems, from data collection and training to deployment and monitoring.

- **Leveraging Advanced Cryptographic Techniques:** Emerging cryptographic techniques, such as homomorphic encryption (which allows computation on encrypted data without decrypting it), can provide new ways to protect data privacy while maintaining utility for AI applications.

Conclusion: Embracing Data and Privacy-Based Protection in AI Development

Data and privacy-based protection strategies, such as advanced data masking and anonymization techniques, offer valuable tools for safeguarding AI-generated works and maintaining compliance with data protection laws. By integrating these approaches into AI development, organizations can enhance privacy, security, and trust while promoting ethical and responsible use of AI technologies.

Chapter 10:

Future Impacts, Strategies, and Ethical Considerations for Managing AI-Generated Works

Forecasts on Regulatory Evolution in the United States and Internationally

As artificial intelligence (AI) continues to transform the creative, technological, and commercial landscapes, there is a growing recognition that existing legal frameworks, particularly in the realm of intellectual property (IP), need to evolve to address the unique challenges posed by AI-generated works. This section explores the potential regulatory changes in the United States and globally, examining trends in national and regional policies, and the roles of international organizations in shaping a coherent, adaptive, and equitable legal environment for AI-generated content.

Trends in U.S. Regulatory Changes: Expected Reforms of the Copyright Act and Discussions on a New "AI Act"

The United States has traditionally been a leader in intellectual property law, with frameworks that have influenced global standards. However, the rapid advancement of AI technologies and the rise of AI-generated content have highlighted significant gaps in the existing legal structure. Policymakers, industry leaders, and legal scholars are currently discussing potential reforms to address these challenges, focusing on updates to the Copyright Act and the introduction of new legislation, such as a proposed "AI Act."

Expected Reforms of the Copyright Act

The U.S. Copyright Act of 1976, which governs copyright protection, was written long before the advent of AI technologies. The law is based on the assumption that all copyrighted works have a human author, and it does not address the complexities introduced by AI-generated works.

- **Clarifying Authorship and Originality Requirements:** One of the key areas of expected reform involves clarifying the requirements for authorship and originality as they pertain to AI-generated works. Current law requires that a work be an original creation by a human author to qualify for copyright protection. Reforms may explore new definitions of authorship that can accommodate works generated with AI assistance or autonomously by AI systems, possibly recognizing human oversight or control as a criterion for protection.

- **Establishing New Categories for AI-Generated Works:** Another proposed change is to establish new copyright categories specifically for AI-generated works. These categories could provide different levels of protection based on the degree of human involvement, the nature of the AI's contribution, and the intended use of the work. For example, works created with significant human guidance might receive similar protections to traditional works, while fully autonomous AI-generated content might receive a more limited scope of protection.

- **Adjusting the Duration of Copyright Protection:** Given the challenges of applying traditional copyright rules to AI-generated works, policymakers are considering adjusting the duration of protection for such works. Shorter copyright terms might be introduced for AI-generated content to balance the rights of creators with the public interest in access to creative works, ensuring that the legal framework encourages innovation while avoiding perpetual monopolies.

Discussions on a New "AI Act"

In addition to amending existing laws, there is growing discussion around the need for a new "AI Act" in the United States, similar to legislative initiatives underway in other regions, such as the European Union. The proposed "AI Act" could provide a comprehensive legal framework specifically designed to regulate AI technologies, including those that generate creative content.

- **Establishing Standards for AI Transparency and Accountability:** A key component of the AI Act would be setting standards for transparency and accountability in the use of AI systems. This could include requirements for disclosing when AI has been used to create content, providing explanations of AI decision-making processes, and ensuring that AI outputs do not infringe on existing IP rights or ethical guidelines.
- **Regulating High-Risk AI Applications:** The AI Act could introduce specific regulations for high-risk AI applications, such as deepfakes, synthetic media, and AI-generated journalism, which have significant implications for privacy, security, and public trust. These regulations might include requirements for labeling AI-generated content, restrictions on certain uses of AI, and penalties for misuse.
- **Creating a Legal Framework for AI Liability:** The AI Act could also establish a framework for determining liability in cases where AI-generated works cause harm or infringe upon rights. This might include defining the responsibilities of AI developers, operators, and users, and creating mechanisms for dispute resolution and compensation.
- **Encouraging Ethical AI Development:** To promote ethical AI development, the AI Act could include provisions for fairness, non-discrimination, and human-centric AI design. This could involve mandatory impact assessments, guidelines for AI ethics, and incentives for developing AI technologies that align with public values and interests.

Developments in Europe, Asia, and Other Key Markets: Policy Comparisons and Cooperative Initiatives

As AI-generated works proliferate globally, countries and regions are developing their own policies and regulatory approaches to manage the unique challenges posed by these technologies. Europe, Asia, and other key markets are taking distinct yet often complementary approaches, reflecting their unique legal traditions, economic priorities, and cultural values.

Europe: The AI Act and Updates to the Copyright Directive

The European Union (EU) is at the forefront of regulating AI technologies, with the proposed AI Act representing one of the most comprehensive attempts to address the ethical, legal, and technical challenges posed by AI.

- **The EU AI Act:** The proposed EU AI Act aims to create a harmonized framework for AI regulation across member states, categorizing AI applications into different risk levels (e.g., minimal, limited, high, and unacceptable risk) and imposing varying levels of regulatory obligations accordingly.
  - **Impact on AI-Generated Works:** The AI Act includes provisions that could impact AI-generated works, such as transparency requirements for AI systems, obligations for high-risk AI applications, and restrictions on certain types of AI-generated content that could pose risks to public safety or fundamental rights.
  - **Alignment with Existing IP Laws:** The AI Act will need to align with existing EU IP laws, such as the Copyright Directive, which was updated in 2019 to address some digital challenges but did not specifically cover AI-generated works. Further updates to the Copyright Directive or new legislation may be needed to ensure consistency between the AI Act and IP protection.
- **Digital Single Market Strategy and Copyright Reform:** The EU's Digital Single Market Strategy includes ongoing reforms to modernize copyright law in the digital age. These reforms may explore new definitions of authorship, adjust the scope of protection for AI-generated works, and promote cross-border cooperation on IP enforcement.

Asia: Diverse Approaches to AI Regulation

Asian countries, including China, Japan, and South Korea, are developing their own frameworks for managing AI-generated works, reflecting diverse legal systems and regulatory philosophies.

- **China:** China has emerged as a leader in AI development and regulation, with a proactive approach to managing both the opportunities and risks of AI technologies.
  - ○ **China's AI Policy Framework:** China's National AI Development Plan emphasizes both innovation and regulation, with specific guidelines on ethical AI development, transparency, and accountability. While China has yet to implement a comprehensive AI-specific law like the EU's AI Act, it has introduced sector-specific regulations that impact AI-generated content, such as rules on deepfakes and news synthesis.
  - ○ **IP Protection and AI:** China's IP laws are evolving to address AI-generated works, with recent reforms to the Copyright Law emphasizing the need for clarity in ownership and authorship issues related to AI. The Chinese government is actively promoting international cooperation on AI standards and IP protection.
- **Japan and South Korea:** Japan and South Korea are also exploring new regulations for AI-generated works, balancing innovation with ethical considerations.
  - ○ **Japan's AI Strategy:** Japan's AI strategy focuses on promoting AI innovation while addressing ethical concerns, particularly in the context of data privacy and security. Japan is considering updates to its copyright laws to clarify the status of AI-generated works and the rights of AI developers and users.
  - ○ **South Korea's AI Framework:** South Korea is developing an AI regulatory framework that emphasizes transparency, fairness, and accountability. South Korea's IP Office is also studying the implications of AI on patent and copyright laws, with a view to introducing reforms that align with global standards.

Other Key Markets: Policy Comparisons and Cooperative Initiatives

Beyond the U.S., Europe, and Asia, other key markets are also shaping the future of AI regulation and IP protection.

- **Australia and Canada:** Australia and Canada are exploring how to adapt their IP laws to address the challenges of AI-generated works, with an emphasis on balancing innovation with protection. Both countries are active participants in international discussions on AI standards and IP reform.
- **Latin America and Africa:** In Latin America and Africa, regulatory frameworks for AI are still in the early stages of development. However, there is growing interest in leveraging AI technologies for economic development and innovation while ensuring ethical and responsible use. Regional organizations are beginning to explore cooperative initiatives to develop shared standards and policies.
- **Cooperative Initiatives and Global Policy Networks:** As countries and regions develop their own regulatory approaches, there is a growing need for cooperative initiatives and global policy networks to ensure consistency, interoperability, and mutual recognition of standards. International organizations, such as the OECD, G20, and UN, are fostering dialogue and collaboration on AI policy, including IP protection and ethical considerations.

Role of International Organizations: World Intellectual Property Organization (WIPO), European Patent Office (EPO), and Others

International organizations play a critical role in shaping global standards and fostering cooperation on the regulation of AI-generated works. These organizations provide forums for dialogue, develop guidelines and model laws, and promote harmonization across jurisdictions.

World Intellectual Property Organization (WIPO)

- **WIPO's Role in AI and IP Policy:** As the leading global organization for intellectual property, WIPO is actively engaged in discussions on the intersection of AI and IP. WIPO's activities include:
  - **Developing Global Standards and Guidelines:** WIPO is working to develop global standards and guidelines for

protecting AI-generated works, including new definitions of authorship and originality, criteria for patentability, and frameworks for managing rights and licensing.

- o **Facilitating International Dialogue and Cooperation:** WIPO convenes member states, industry stakeholders, and experts to discuss challenges and opportunities related to AI-generated works. These discussions aim to promote international cooperation and build consensus on best practices and policy approaches.
- o **Capacity Building and Technical Assistance:** WIPO provides capacity building and technical assistance to member states, helping them develop and implement effective IP policies for AI-generated content.

European Patent Office (EPO) and Other Regional Organizations

- **EPO's Focus on AI-Related Patents:** The European Patent Office (EPO) is at the forefront of examining AI-related patents, developing guidelines for patent examiners, and engaging in dialogue with stakeholders to address the unique challenges of AI patentability.
  - o **Guidelines for AI and Machine Learning Patents:** The EPO has issued guidelines for the examination of AI and machine learning inventions, clarifying the requirements for novelty, inventive step, and industrial applicability. These guidelines help ensure consistency and transparency in the patenting process.
  - o **Collaboration with Other Patent Offices:** The EPO collaborates with other patent offices, such as the USPTO and the Japan Patent Office (JPO), to harmonize patent examination practices for AI-related inventions and promote cross-border recognition of patents.
- **Other Regional Organizations:** Other regional organizations, such as the African Regional Intellectual Property Organization (ARIPO) and the Latin American Intellectual Property Association (ASIPI), are also beginning to engage with the

challenges of AI-generated works, promoting regional dialogue and cooperation on IP protection and regulatory innovation.

Moving Forward: Building a Global Framework for AI Regulation and IP Protection

To manage the complexities of AI-generated works effectively, international organizations and national governments must work together to build a global framework that balances innovation with protection, fosters ethical AI development, and ensures fair access to AI technologies:

- **Promoting Harmonization and Interoperability:** Harmonizing legal standards and ensuring interoperability across jurisdictions is essential to provide consistent protection and minimize conflicts. This could involve developing model laws, best practices, and guidelines that countries can adapt to their national contexts.
- **Encouraging Multilateral Cooperation:** Multilateral cooperation through international organizations like WIPO, the OECD, and the UN will be crucial in fostering dialogue, sharing knowledge, and building consensus on global standards for AI-generated works.
- **Adapting to Future Developments:** As AI technologies continue to evolve, legal frameworks must remain flexible and adaptive to address new challenges and opportunities. Ongoing engagement with stakeholders, regular reviews of policies, and openness to innovation will be key to developing a robust and future-proof regulatory environment.

Strategies for Innovators, Companies, and Creators Using AI

As the use of artificial intelligence (AI) becomes more widespread in creative and technological fields, innovators, companies, and creators must adopt effective strategies to navigate the evolving legal landscape, protect their interests, and maximize the value of AI-generated works. This section outlines best practices for creating and registering AI-generated works, drafting innovative contracts and licensing agreements, and fostering collaborations between researchers, lawyers, and technology experts to address the unique challenges posed by AI.

Best Practices for Creating and Registering AI-Generated Works

Given the uncertainties and complexities surrounding the legal status of AI-generated works, creators and companies should follow best practices to ensure they are protected under current and future legal frameworks. These practices help establish ownership, mitigate risks, and enhance the marketability of AI-generated content.

Documentation and Record Keeping

- **Maintain Detailed Records of Creation Processes:** Document every step of the creation process, including the role of the AI system, the input data used, the level of human involvement, and any modifications made to the AI-generated output. This documentation can help demonstrate the originality of the work, establish authorship or ownership, and provide evidence in case of disputes.
- **Record Human Contributions and Decisions:** Clearly record the contributions made by human authors or operators, including any decisions that influenced the AI system's output. This is particularly important in jurisdictions that may require some level of human involvement to qualify for copyright or patent protection.
- **Capture AI System Details:** Keep detailed records of the AI system itself, including the algorithms used, training data sources, and any proprietary technologies involved. This information can be crucial for demonstrating that the work is original and does not infringe on existing IP rights.

Choose the Appropriate Type of Protection

- **Evaluate Different Forms of IP Protection:** Assess whether the AI-generated work is best protected under copyright, patent, trademark, trade secret, or a combination of these. Consider the nature of the work, the potential market, and the level of protection required. For example, AI-generated software may benefit from patent protection, while an AI-generated design might be more suitable for copyright or trademark protection.

- **Register with Relevant Authorities:** Where possible, register AI-generated works with national or regional IP offices to secure formal protection. Even in cases where the legal status of AI-generated works is unclear, registration can provide a formal record that may be useful in establishing ownership or priority.

Use Alternative Registration Mechanisms

- **Leverage Blockchain for Proof of Authorship:** Consider using blockchain technology as an alternative mechanism for registering AI-generated works. Blockchain can provide a secure, transparent, and immutable record of authorship and creation, which can be useful in establishing ownership and licensing rights.

- **Utilize Open Source and Creative Commons Licenses:** For certain types of AI-generated content, especially those intended for public use or collaborative development, consider using open source or Creative Commons licenses. These licenses can help manage rights while promoting wider dissemination and use of the content.

How to Draft Innovative Contracts and Licensing Agreements: Key Clauses and Specific Conditions

Contracts and licensing agreements are critical tools for managing the rights and responsibilities associated with AI-generated works. Given the unique nature of these works, innovators and companies should draft agreements that address specific challenges and anticipate potential legal developments.

Key Clauses for AI-Generated Works

- **Define Authorship and Ownership Clearly:** Specify the authorship and ownership of the AI-generated work, including the roles of human creators, AI developers, and operators. Clarify who holds the rights to the work, how those rights are to be exercised, and what happens in the event of a dispute.

- **Address AI-Specific Issues:** Include clauses that address AI-specific issues, such as the transparency of AI decision-making, the use of training data, and the ethical considerations involved in using AI. For example, contracts could require disclosure of any biases in the AI system or ensure compliance with data protection laws.
- **Set Out Usage and Licensing Terms:** Clearly define the scope of the license, including the permitted uses of the AI-generated work, geographic and temporal limitations, and any restrictions on modifications or sublicensing. Consider including specific terms for high-risk applications, such as deepfakes or synthetic media.

Specific Conditions to Include in Licensing Agreements

- **Royalty and Revenue-Sharing Arrangements:** Include detailed provisions on royalty and revenue-sharing arrangements, particularly in cases where multiple parties contribute to or have a stake in the AI-generated work. Specify how royalties are calculated, distributed, and reported, and consider using smart contracts to automate these processes.
- **Indemnification and Liability Clauses:** Address the potential risks associated with AI-generated works, including IP infringement, data privacy breaches, and other legal liabilities. Include indemnification clauses to protect against claims and specify the responsibilities of each party in case of litigation or regulatory action.
- **Termination and Renewal Terms:** Define the conditions under which the agreement may be terminated or renewed. Consider including provisions for automatic renewal, non-renewal notice periods, and termination for breach or failure to comply with specific conditions.

Leveraging Smart Contracts for AI Licensing

- **Use Smart Contracts for Automation:** Leverage smart contracts on blockchain platforms to automate key elements of licensing agreements, such as royalty payments, rights transfers, and compliance monitoring. Smart contracts can provide transparency, reduce administrative costs, and ensure that terms are executed promptly and accurately.

- **Ensure Smart Contracts Are Legally Enforceable:** When using smart contracts, ensure that they are legally enforceable in the relevant jurisdictions. Include traditional contract elements, such as signatures or digital authentication methods, to enhance enforceability.

Collaborations Between Researchers, Lawyers, and Technology Experts: Creating Interdisciplinary Task Forces

To effectively manage AI-generated works and navigate the evolving legal landscape, innovators, companies, and creators should foster collaborations between researchers, lawyers, and technology experts. Interdisciplinary task forces can help develop best practices, anticipate legal developments, and ensure compliance with regulatory requirements.

Benefits of Interdisciplinary Collaboration

- **Bridging Knowledge Gaps:** Collaborations between researchers, lawyers, and technology experts help bridge the knowledge gaps that often exist between these disciplines. Lawyers can better understand the technical complexities of AI, while technologists gain insights into the legal and regulatory implications of their work.
- **Enhancing Compliance and Risk Management:** By working together, interdisciplinary teams can develop strategies to ensure compliance with current laws and anticipate future legal changes. This collaboration can help identify potential risks early, mitigate legal liabilities, and develop more robust IP protection strategies.
- **Driving Innovation and Ethical AI Use:** Interdisciplinary task forces can drive innovation by fostering a deeper understanding of both the opportunities and challenges of AI. They can develop guidelines for ethical AI use, promote best practices, and advocate for legal reforms that support responsible AI development.

Strategies for Forming Interdisciplinary Task Forces

- **Identify Key Stakeholders and Areas of Expertise:** Identify the key stakeholders who should be involved in the task force, including AI developers, data scientists, IP lawyers, privacy experts, ethicists, and representatives from relevant regulatory bodies. Define the areas of expertise needed and ensure a balanced representation of technical and legal perspectives.

- **Develop Clear Objectives and Action Plans:** Establish clear objectives for the task force, such as developing best practices for AI-generated works, monitoring legal developments, or advocating for regulatory changes. Create an action plan with specific goals, timelines, and deliverables to guide the task force's work.

- **Foster Open Communication and Knowledge Sharing:** Encourage open communication and knowledge sharing among task force members. Use regular meetings, workshops, and collaborative platforms to facilitate discussions, exchange insights, and build trust and cooperation.

Examples of Successful Interdisciplinary Collaborations

- **Industry Consortia and Working Groups:** Examples of successful interdisciplinary collaborations include industry consortia and working groups focused on AI ethics, standards, and IP. Organizations like the Partnership on AI, the AI Ethics Lab, and the Creative Commons AI Initiative bring together experts from various fields to address the challenges and opportunities of AI.

- **Academic and Research Collaborations:** Universities and research institutions are increasingly partnering with industry and legal experts to study the impact of AI on IP law and develop new frameworks for managing AI-generated works. Collaborative projects such as the Berkman Klein Center's research on AI and copyright law exemplify these efforts.

Strategies for Innovators, Companies, and Creators Using AI

As the use of artificial intelligence (AI) becomes more widespread in creative and technological fields, innovators, companies, and creators

239

must adopt effective strategies to navigate the evolving legal landscape, protect their interests, and maximize the value of AI-generated works. This section outlines best practices for creating and registering AI-generated works, drafting innovative contracts and licensing agreements, and fostering collaborations between researchers, lawyers, and technology experts to address the unique challenges posed by AI.

Best Practices for Creating and Registering AI-Generated Works

Given the uncertainties and complexities surrounding the legal status of AI-generated works, creators and companies should follow best practices to ensure they are protected under current and future legal frameworks. These practices help establish ownership, mitigate risks, and enhance the marketability of AI-generated content.

Documentation and Record Keeping

- **Maintain Detailed Records of Creation Processes:** Document every step of the creation process, including the role of the AI system, the input data used, the level of human involvement, and any modifications made to the AI-generated output. This documentation can help demonstrate the originality of the work, establish authorship or ownership, and provide evidence in case of disputes.

- **Record Human Contributions and Decisions:** Clearly record the contributions made by human authors or operators, including any decisions that influenced the AI system's output. This is particularly important in jurisdictions that may require some level of human involvement to qualify for copyright or patent protection.

- **Capture AI System Details:** Keep detailed records of the AI system itself, including the algorithms used, training data sources, and any proprietary technologies involved. This information can be crucial for demonstrating that the work is original and does not infringe on existing IP rights.

Choose the Appropriate Type of Protection

- **Evaluate Different Forms of IP Protection:** Assess whether the AI-generated work is best protected under copyright, patent,

240

trademark, trade secret, or a combination of these. Consider the nature of the work, the potential market, and the level of protection required. For example, AI-generated software may benefit from patent protection, while an AI-generated design might be more suitable for copyright or trademark protection.

- **Register with Relevant Authorities:** Where possible, register AI-generated works with national or regional IP offices to secure formal protection. Even in cases where the legal status of AI-generated works is unclear, registration can provide a formal record that may be useful in establishing ownership or priority.

Use Alternative Registration Mechanisms

- **Leverage Blockchain for Proof of Authorship:** Consider using blockchain technology as an alternative mechanism for registering AI-generated works. Blockchain can provide a secure, transparent, and immutable record of authorship and creation, which can be useful in establishing ownership and licensing rights.
- **Utilize Open Source and Creative Commons Licenses:** For certain types of AI-generated content, especially those intended for public use or collaborative development, consider using open source or Creative Commons licenses. These licenses can help manage rights while promoting wider dissemination and use of the content.

How to Draft Innovative Contracts and Licensing Agreements: Key Clauses and Specific Conditions

Contracts and licensing agreements are critical tools for managing the rights and responsibilities associated with AI-generated works. Given the unique nature of these works, innovators and companies should draft agreements that address specific challenges and anticipate potential legal developments.

Key Clauses for AI-Generated Works

- **Define Authorship and Ownership Clearly:** Specify the authorship and ownership of the AI-generated work, including the roles of human creators, AI developers, and operators. Clarify who holds the rights to the work, how those rights are to be exercised, and what happens in the event of a dispute.

- **Address AI-Specific Issues:** Include clauses that address AI-specific issues, such as the transparency of AI decision-making, the use of training data, and the ethical considerations involved in using AI. For example, contracts could require disclosure of any biases in the AI system or ensure compliance with data protection laws.

- **Set Out Usage and Licensing Terms:** Clearly define the scope of the license, including the permitted uses of the AI-generated work, geographic and temporal limitations, and any restrictions on modifications or sublicensing. Consider including specific terms for high-risk applications, such as deepfakes or synthetic media.

Specific Conditions to Include in Licensing Agreements

- **Royalty and Revenue-Sharing Arrangements:** Include detailed provisions on royalty and revenue-sharing arrangements, particularly in cases where multiple parties contribute to or have a stake in the AI-generated work. Specify how royalties are calculated, distributed, and reported, and consider using smart contracts to automate these processes.

- **Indemnification and Liability Clauses:** Address the potential risks associated with AI-generated works, including IP infringement, data privacy breaches, and other legal liabilities. Include indemnification clauses to protect against claims and specify the responsibilities of each party in case of litigation or regulatory action.

- **Termination and Renewal Terms:** Define the conditions under which the agreement may be terminated or renewed. Consider including provisions for automatic renewal, non-renewal notice periods, and termination for breach or failure to comply with specific conditions.

Leveraging Smart Contracts for AI Licensing

- **Use Smart Contracts for Automation:** Leverage smart contracts on blockchain platforms to automate key elements of licensing agreements, such as royalty payments, rights transfers, and compliance monitoring. Smart contracts can provide transparency, reduce administrative costs, and ensure that terms are executed promptly and accurately.
- **Ensure Smart Contracts Are Legally Enforceable:** When using smart contracts, ensure that they are legally enforceable in the relevant jurisdictions. Include traditional contract elements, such as signatures or digital authentication methods, to enhance enforceability.

Collaborations Between Researchers, Lawyers, and Technology Experts: Creating Interdisciplinary Task Forces

To effectively manage AI-generated works and navigate the evolving legal landscape, innovators, companies, and creators should foster collaborations between researchers, lawyers, and technology experts. Interdisciplinary task forces can help develop best practices, anticipate legal developments, and ensure compliance with regulatory requirements.

Benefits of Interdisciplinary Collaboration

- **Bridging Knowledge Gaps:** Collaborations between researchers, lawyers, and technology experts help bridge the knowledge gaps that often exist between these disciplines. Lawyers can better understand the technical complexities of AI, while technologists gain insights into the legal and regulatory implications of their work.
- **Enhancing Compliance and Risk Management:** By working together, interdisciplinary teams can develop strategies to ensure compliance with current laws and anticipate future legal changes. This collaboration can help identify potential risks early, mitigate legal liabilities, and develop more robust IP protection strategies.
- **Driving Innovation and Ethical AI Use:** Interdisciplinary task forces can drive innovation by fostering a deeper understanding

of both the opportunities and challenges of AI. They can develop guidelines for ethical AI use, promote best practices, and advocate for legal reforms that support responsible AI development.

Strategies for Forming Interdisciplinary Task Forces

- **Identify Key Stakeholders and Areas of Expertise:** Identify the key stakeholders who should be involved in the task force, including AI developers, data scientists, IP lawyers, privacy experts, ethicists, and representatives from relevant regulatory bodies. Define the areas of expertise needed and ensure a balanced representation of technical and legal perspectives.

- **Develop Clear Objectives and Action Plans:** Establish clear objectives for the task force, such as developing best practices for AI-generated works, monitoring legal developments, or advocating for regulatory changes. Create an action plan with specific goals, timelines, and deliverables to guide the task force's work.

- **Foster Open Communication and Knowledge Sharing:** Encourage open communication and knowledge sharing among task force members. Use regular meetings, workshops, and collaborative platforms to facilitate discussions, exchange insights, and build trust and cooperation.

Examples of Successful Interdisciplinary Collaborations

- **Industry Consortia and Working Groups:** Examples of successful interdisciplinary collaborations include industry consortia and working groups focused on AI ethics, standards, and IP. Organizations like the Partnership on AI, the AI Ethics Lab, and the Creative Commons AI Initiative bring together experts from various fields to address the challenges and opportunities of AI.

- **Academic and Research Collaborations:** Universities and research institutions are increasingly partnering with industry and legal experts to study the impact of AI on IP law and develop new frameworks for managing AI-generated works.

Collaborative projects such as the Berkman Klein Center's research on AI and copyright law exemplify these efforts.

Moving Forward: Building Effective Interdisciplinary Partnerships

- **Encourage Public-Private Partnerships:** Public-private partnerships can help bridge the gap between policy development and technological innovation. Governments, academic institutions, and private companies should work together to develop comprehensive strategies for managing AI-generated works. These partnerships can facilitate the sharing of resources, knowledge, and expertise, ensuring that all stakeholders are involved in shaping the future legal landscape for AI.

- **Develop Joint Training Programs and Workshops:** To build effective interdisciplinary collaborations, consider developing joint training programs and workshops that bring together professionals from different fields. These programs can help lawyers understand the technical aspects of AI, while technologists gain insights into the legal, ethical, and regulatory implications of their work. Workshops can also serve as forums for brainstorming, problem-solving, and developing innovative approaches to managing AI-generated works.

- **Create Multidisciplinary Research Initiatives:** Encourage the formation of multidisciplinary research initiatives that focus on the intersection of AI, law, ethics, and technology. These initiatives can explore critical issues such as the implications of AI-generated works for IP law, the ethical challenges of AI use in creative industries, and the potential need for new regulatory frameworks. By fostering collaboration between researchers and practitioners, these initiatives can contribute to the development of evidence-based policies and best practices.

- **Leverage Technology for Collaboration:** Utilize digital collaboration tools and platforms to facilitate communication and coordination among interdisciplinary teams. These tools can help streamline workflows, manage projects, and enable real-time collaboration across different locations. Additionally, AI-driven collaboration tools can enhance productivity and support

245

decision-making by providing insights and recommendations based on data analysis.

- **Establish Ongoing Dialogue with Policymakers:** Interdisciplinary task forces should maintain an ongoing dialogue with policymakers to ensure that their work aligns with legislative developments and regulatory requirements. Engaging with policymakers can also provide valuable opportunities to advocate for legal reforms, share insights from research and practice, and influence the direction of future regulations related to AI-generated works.

- **Promote Ethical Standards and Guidelines:** As part of their work, interdisciplinary task forces should promote the development and adoption of ethical standards and guidelines for AI-generated works. These standards can help ensure that AI technologies are used responsibly and that the rights of creators, consumers, and other stakeholders are protected. By establishing clear ethical guidelines, task forces can contribute to the development of a more trustworthy and transparent AI ecosystem.

- **Measure and Evaluate the Impact of Collaborative Efforts:** To ensure the effectiveness of interdisciplinary partnerships, it is essential to measure and evaluate the impact of collaborative efforts. Regular assessments can help identify areas for improvement, track progress toward goals, and demonstrate the value of interdisciplinary collaboration in managing AI-generated works. Feedback from participants and stakeholders can also provide insights into the success of these initiatives and guide future efforts.

Ethical and Social Considerations on Using AI for Creative Works

As AI technologies become increasingly integrated into creative processes, they raise important ethical and social questions. While AI has the potential to enhance human creativity and expand access to cultural content, it also poses significant risks, such as content homogenization, the erosion of human authorship, and the concentration of creative power in the hands of a few. This section examines the ethical and social considerations of using AI for creative works, focusing on its impact on human creativity and cultural diversity, the balance between AI autonomy and human control, and the need for social justice and equitable access to technology.

Impact on Human Creativity and Cultural Diversity: Risks of Content Homogenization

AI has the potential to transform creative industries by generating content quickly, efficiently, and at scale. However, there are concerns that the widespread use of AI in creative processes could lead to homogenization of content, reducing diversity and stifling human creativity.

Risks of Content Homogenization

- **Algorithmic Bias and Repetitiveness:** AI models are typically trained on large datasets that reflect existing patterns, trends, and biases in the data. When these models generate creative works, they tend to reproduce these patterns, potentially leading to a lack of originality and diversity in the output. For example, AI-generated music, literature, or art may rely on common themes or motifs present in the training data, resulting in repetitive and formulaic content.

- **Reduction in Cultural Diversity:** The use of AI in creative processes could undermine cultural diversity by favoring dominant cultural narratives and aesthetics that are prevalent in the training data. This might marginalize minority cultures and perspectives, reducing the representation of diverse voices and expressions in creative industries. As AI-generated content becomes more common, there is a risk that culturally specific and unique works could be overshadowed by more homogenized outputs.

- **Impact on Human Creativity:** The increasing reliance on AI tools for content creation may discourage human creativity and experimentation. If creators perceive AI as a faster or cheaper alternative, they may be less inclined to take creative risks or explore novel ideas. Over time, this could diminish the value of human ingenuity and lead to a more standardized and less vibrant cultural landscape.

Strategies to Mitigate Content Homogenization

- **Promoting Diversity in AI Training Data:** To prevent content homogenization, developers should strive to include diverse and representative datasets in AI training processes. This involves incorporating a wide range of cultural, social, and historical perspectives to ensure that AI-generated content reflects the richness and diversity of human experience.
- **Encouraging Human-AI Collaboration:** Rather than replacing human creativity, AI should be seen as a tool that complements and enhances it. Encouraging collaboration between AI and human creators can lead to more innovative and original works, combining the strengths of both AI capabilities and human intuition, emotion, and imagination.
- **Implementing Ethical Guidelines for AI Content Creation:** Developing and enforcing ethical guidelines for AI content creation can help preserve cultural diversity and promote originality. These guidelines could include principles for avoiding bias, ensuring fairness, and protecting the integrity of cultural expressions in AI-generated works.

AI Autonomy vs. Human Control: Issues of Moral Authorship and Human Rights

The growing autonomy of AI in generating creative content raises profound ethical questions about authorship, control, and the rights of creators and consumers. The balance between AI autonomy and human control is central to ensuring that AI is used responsibly in creative contexts.

Moral Authorship and Ownership

- **Challenges to Traditional Notions of Authorship:** AI-generated works challenge traditional notions of authorship and ownership, which have historically been grounded in human creativity and intent. If AI systems autonomously create works with little or no human input, questions arise about who, if anyone, should be credited as the author. This has implications for moral rights, such as the right of attribution, the right to object to derogatory treatment, and the right to the integrity of the work.

- **Reconsidering Copyright Frameworks:** Existing copyright frameworks are not well-suited to address the complexities of AI-generated works. There is a need to reconsider how copyright laws define authorship, originality, and ownership in the context of AI, and to explore new legal models that recognize the role of AI in the creative process while maintaining the moral rights of human creators.

Human Rights and Ethical Considerations

- **AI and Free Expression:** AI-generated works have implications for free expression, particularly if AI systems are used to create content that influences public opinion, disseminates misinformation, or manipulates behavior. Ensuring that AI-generated content respects human rights, including the right to freedom of expression and access to information, is essential to maintaining democratic values and social trust.

- **Accountability for Harmful AI Outputs:** In cases where AI-generated works cause harm, such as offensive or defamatory content, determining accountability can be challenging. Policymakers and stakeholders must address questions of liability and responsibility for AI outputs, particularly when those outputs infringe on human rights or violate ethical standards.

Balancing AI Autonomy with Human Control

- **Implementing Transparent AI Governance:** To balance AI autonomy with human control, it is essential to implement transparent governance frameworks that set clear rules for the use of AI in creative processes. These frameworks should define the roles and responsibilities of AI developers, operators, and users, and ensure that human oversight is maintained, particularly in high-risk applications.

- **Promoting Human-Centric AI Design:** AI systems should be designed to support and augment human creativity, rather than replace it. Human-centric AI design principles emphasize the importance of keeping humans in the loop, ensuring that AI tools remain subject to human judgment, supervision, and ethical considerations.

Social Justice and Accessibility: Avoiding Concentration of Creative Power and Promoting Equitable Access to Technologies

The deployment of AI in creative industries has the potential to democratize access to creative tools and platforms. However, there is also a risk that AI could exacerbate existing inequalities and concentrate creative power in the hands of a few, leading to social injustice and reduced accessibility.

Avoiding Concentration of Creative Power

- **Monopolization of AI Tools and Data:** The development and deployment of AI technologies are often controlled by a small number of powerful companies that have access to vast amounts of data, computational resources, and technical expertise. This concentration of power can limit access to AI tools for smaller creators, startups, and underserved communities, reinforcing existing inequalities in the creative industries.
- **Barriers to Entry for Independent Creators:** High costs associated with AI technologies, such as purchasing software licenses, accessing high-quality training data, and utilizing cloud computing resources, can create barriers to entry for independent creators and small businesses. This may restrict the diversity of voices in creative fields and limit opportunities for innovation.

Promoting Equitable Access to AI Technologies

- **Developing Open Source AI Tools and Platforms:** Promoting the development and dissemination of open source AI tools and platforms can help democratize access to AI technologies. By making AI tools freely available, open source initiatives can empower more creators to leverage AI in their work, fostering innovation and diversity in creative industries.

- **Encouraging Public and Private Investments in AI Accessibility:** Governments, non-profits, and private sector organizations should invest in initiatives that promote equitable access to AI technologies, particularly for marginalized and underserved communities. This could include funding for AI education and training programs, support for small businesses and independent creators, and the development of affordable and accessible AI tools.
- **Creating Inclusive AI Policies:** Policymakers should develop inclusive AI policies that prioritize social justice and accessibility. These policies could include incentives for companies to share data and resources, support for community-based AI projects, and measures to ensure that AI-generated content reflects diverse perspectives and serves the public interest.

Supporting Ethical AI Practices in Creative Industries

- **Establishing Fair Compensation Models:** To promote fairness and equity, stakeholders should explore new compensation models for AI-generated works that reflect the value contributed by both human and machine. This could include revenue-sharing agreements, licensing fees, or royalties that recognize the roles of multiple contributors, including AI developers and human creators.
- **Advocating for Responsible AI Use:** Advocacy groups, creative communities, and industry organizations should promote responsible AI use, encouraging practices that prioritize human creativity, cultural diversity, and social justice. This could involve developing ethical guidelines, conducting impact assessments, and engaging in public discourse about the role of AI in creative industries.

Moving Forward: Ensuring Ethical and Inclusive Use of AI in Creative Fields

To ensure that AI is used ethically and inclusively in creative fields, stakeholders should:

- **Promote Inclusive Innovation:** Encourage innovation that benefits all members of society, rather than just a privileged few. This includes investing in diverse AI talent, fostering inclusive research and development, and supporting projects that address social and cultural needs.
- **Foster Global Dialogue on AI Ethics:** Engage in global dialogue on the ethical use of AI in creative industries, bringing together diverse voices and perspectives from around the world. This dialogue should aim to build consensus on best practices, address ethical dilemmas, and develop shared principles for AI governance.
- **Monitor and Evaluate Ethical Impacts:** Continuously monitor and evaluate the ethical and social impacts of AI in creative fields. This includes assessing how AI-generated works affect cultural diversity, human rights, and social justice, and making necessary adjustments to policies, practices, and regulations.